D1062831

# LATIN HYMNS SUNG AT THE CHURCH OF SAINT HUGH LETCHWORTH

# LATIN
# HYMNS

SUNG AT THE CHURCH
OF SAINT HUGH LETCHWORTH
ARRANGED & TRANSLATED
BY A·F

**ROMAN CATHOLIC BOOKS**
P.O. Box 255
Harrison, NY 10528

ISBN 0-912141-13-1

# PREFACE

THIS book is meant to serve a practical purpose. In our church on Sunday evening, during and after Benediction, we sing various Latin hymns or antiphons. Since Compline hardly ever changes, an excellent way to remember the feast or season is to sing the Vesper hymn of the day, with its versicle and collect, at Benediction. We have also a number of beautiful hymns about the Blessed Sacrament, our Lady, the Church, and so on. But if people do not understand what is sung, to them all this is lost. To find each hymn and antiphon you would need quite a large collection of books. So I have gathered together all the hymns and chants which we usually sing, with a double purpose. First, that anyone who knows the tune may join the singers; secondly, that those who do not sing may be able to follow, to know what is being sung. Every text has an English translation on the opposite page. If anyone does not understand Latin, he can use the translation as his own prayer and so join in intention with those who sing.

A great number of the hymns are taken from the Roman breviary. Many of these were altered in 1629, with the idea of making them agree better with the laws of classical Latin poetry. Everyone now admits that this was a mistake. Much of the beauty of the older forms was lost and the hymns did not really become classical. We have reason to hope that the present reform of the breviary will also give us back the old form of the hymns. But meanwhile it seems necessary to keep the later text. This is the one best known, it is given in all hymn-books and is still the only authorized form. Only in one case have we printed the older text of a hymn, number 57, 'Vrbs Ierusalem.' The modern form of this begins: 'Cælestis urbs Ierusalem.' But in this case the people who changed it in the seventeenth century did not even keep its metre; so the later version cannot be sung to the old, exceedingly beautiful tune. Other hymns and chants in this book are taken from approved sources. As this is not a book in which to study the history of Latin hymns, I have given only a slight indication of their origin. Their history may be read in Daniel: 'Thesaurus Hymnologicus' (Leipzig, 1855), or, better still, in Dreves: 'Analecta Hymnica' (ib. 1886).

Several of the hymns here printed are not complete. That is the case in the breviary hymns too. Many breviary hymns are really only fragments of very long compositions. It would become tiring to sing ten or twenty verses; nor does there seem any object in filling up pages

with verses which we should never use. So
when the hymn seemed too long I have left out
later verses, taking only those generally sung.
If anyone is interested in the matter, he can
find the full text in the works named.

The translation of number 9, 'Veni, ueni Emmanuel,' is taken from the Arundel Hymn-
Book; that of the Compline hymn, 'Te lucis,'
one of the so-called Ambrosian hymns, is by
E. Caswall, Cong. Orat. (d. 1878). The others
are by me. I have used a few translations in
verse which I made at different times; other-
wise I have written a prose version. After
Dr Neale's beautiful poetic translations of
nearly all our hymns it seems vain for anyone
else to try to rival them. Moreover, since the
English is not meant to be sung, but only to
tell people who do not understand Latin what
the text means, a simple paraphrase in prose is
sufficient. The versions are not always very
literal. Literal translations from Latin hymns
would often look odd in English. I have tried
to give in a readable, generally rhythmic form
the real meaning of the text. At the end of the
book we have added Compline and the Benediction service, so that with the English Hymn-
Book it contains all our usual evening service.
In this book are hymns of all dates, from the
second century to our own time. So even so

slight a collection as this may give some idea of the amazing richness of the treasure the Church possesses in her hymns. There is not and there is never likely to be any religious poetry in the world worthy to be compared with the hymns of the Latin office. Even in their altered forms, which after all leave the ideas and most of the text unchanged, our old Latin hymns are immeasurably more beautiful than any others ever composed. Other religious bodies take all their best hymns in translations from us. It would be a disgrace if we Catholics were the only people who did not appreciate what is our property. And, from every point of view, we of the old Church cannot do better than sing to God as our fathers sang to him during all the long ages behind us. Nor shall we find a better expression of Catholic piety than these words, hallowed by centuries of Catholic use, fragrant with the memory of the saints who wrote them in that golden age when practically all Christendom was Catholic.

A. F.

*Letchworth, Whitsuntide* 1913

# CONTENTS

## V. EASTERTIDE

## VI. WHITSUNTIDE

## VII. THE HOLY EUCHARIST

## VIII. THE BLESSED VIRGIN MARY

## IX. OTHER SAINTS

## X. THE CITY OF GOD

*Nihil obstat:* F. Canonicus Wyndham, *Censor deputatus.*
*Imprimatur:* Edm. Can. Surmont, *Vic. gen. Westmonasterii die* 28 *aprilis* 1913.

# SCHOLAE CANTORVM NOSTRAE

# I. EVENING HYMNS

## I

*Vesper hymn for Sunday from the Breviary,
perhaps by St Gregory I (d. 604)*

LVCIS creátor óptime,
lucem diérum próferens,
primórdiis lucis nouæ
mundi parans oríginem:

2. Qui mane iunctum uésperi
diem uocári præcipis:
illábitur tetrum chaos,
audi preces cum flétibus.

3. Ne mens grauáta crímine
uitæ sit exsul múnere
dum nil perénne cógitat
seséque culpisílligat.

4. Cæléste pulset óstium,
uitále tollat práemium,
uitémus omne nóxium,
purgémus omne péssimum.

5. Præsta, Pater piíssime,
Patríque compar Vnice
cum Spíritu Paráclito
regnans per omne sæculum.

# I. EVENING HYMNS

## I

*Vesper hymn for Sunday from the Breviary, perhaps by St Gregory I (d. 604)*

BLESSED Creator of light who sendest forth the light of day, who didst begin creation by making the first light,

2. Who ordainest morn and even to be called day; the dark night falls, hear the prayers we make with tears.

3. Let not our souls heavy with sin lose the gift of life, lest forgetting eternal things they bind themselves in sin.

4. But let them knock at the door of heaven, let them gain the prize of life. May we flee from crime and cleanse ourselves of evil.

5. Help us, most loving Father, and thou the only-begotten equal to the Father, with the Holy Ghost, reigning for all ages.

### 2

*Attributed to St Ambrose, Bishop of Milan*
*(d. 397)*

O LVX beáta Trínitas
et principális únitas,
iam sol recédit ígneus,
infúnde lumen córdibus.

2. Te mane laudum cármine,
te deprecámur uéspere,
te nostra supplex glória
per cuncta laudat sæcula.

3. Deo Patri sit glória
eiúsque soli Fílio
cum Spíritu Paráclito
nunc et per omne sæculum.

### 3

*A hymn of the 10th cent. to the Holy Trinity*
*(Analecta hymn. xiv, 126)*

T E inuocámus atque adorámus,
teque laudámus, Trínitas beáta,
tu nobis dona scélerum cunctórum
remissiónem.

## 2

*Attributed to St Ambrose, Bishop of Milan*
*(d. 397)*

O BLESSED light, Trinity and Unity, Source of all, now that the bright sun disappears, pour thy light into our hearts.

2. We praise thee with our hymns morning and evening, humbly we glorify thee through all ages.

3. To God the Father be glory and to his only Son, with the Holy Ghost the Comforter, for all ages.

## 3

*A hymn of the 10th cent. to the Holy Trinity*
*(Analecta hymn. XIV, 126)*

THEE we invoke and adore, thee we praise, blessed Trinity; do thou grant to us forgiveness of all sins,

2. Vt ualeámus méntibus deuótis
   ágere dignas tibi quoque laudes
   die ac noĉte, horis et moméntis
   semper dicéntes:

3. Glória ingens sine fine manens
   sit Trinitáti summæ Deitáti
   cunĉta per sæcla, uoce simul una
   cunĉti dicámus      Amen.

4

*By Alcuin of York (d.* 804)

LVMINIS fons, lux et orígo lucis,
   tu pius nostris précibus fauéto,
   luxque peccáti ténebris fugátis
nos petat alma.

2. Ecce transáĉtus labor est diéi,
   nosque te tuti sumus adnuénte:
   en tibi grates ágimus perénnes
   tempus in omne.

3. Solis abscéssus ténebras redúxit:
   ille sol nos irrádiet corúscus
   luce qui fulua fouet angelórum
   ágmina sanĉta.

2. That we may with devout mind give worthy praise to thee day and night, at all hours and moments, saying always:

3. All glory without end be to the Trinity, the high God, for all ages. And together with one voice let us say: Amen.

### 4
### *By Alcuin of York (d. 804)*

FOUNTAIN of light, thyself the light un-
    ending,         [from evil,
  Lord, hear our prayer and, cleansing us
Take away darkness; let thy holy radiance
Shine on thy servants.

Now that the evening brings the end of labour,
Lord, who hast kept us safe in thy protection,
Grateful we offer thee our thanks and worship
Now and at all times.

Since then the daylight fades into the darkness,
Let that sun light us which enlightens always
Choirs of angels in thy holy presence,
Light never failing.

4. Quas dies culpas hodiérna texit
Christe deléto pius atque mitis,
peétus ut puro rútilet nitóre
témpore noétis.

5. Sex dies iustos operémur aétus,
séptimo captent ánimi quiétem,
sint in oétáuo rediuíua nobis
gaúdia uitæ.

5

*'Phos hilaron,' a very old Greek hymn sung
in the Byzantine evening service 'at the light-
ing of the lamps,' attributed to the martyr
Athenogenes (2nd century)*

IVCVNDA lux tu glóriæ,
fons lúminis de lúmine,
beáte Iesu cælitus
a Patre sanéto pródiens.

2. Fulgor diéi lúcidus
solísque lumen óccidit,
et nos ad horam uésperam
te confitémur cántico.

From all the sins which we this day committed
Cleanse thou our conscience, Christ our Lord
and Saviour,
So in the night time we may rest uninjured,
Safe in thy friendship.

Six days we labour, working as thou willest;
Then on the seventh resting by thine order,
We look to that day which at last shall bring us
Rest everlasting.

5

*'Phos hilaron,' a very old Greek hymn sung
in the Byzantine evening service 'at the light-
ing of the lamps,' attributed to the martyr
Athenogenes (2nd century)*

KINDLY light of glory, fount of
light from light, blessed Jesus,
coming from the Father in
heaven,

2. The bright rays of day, the light of
the sun fade; and we at the evening
hour confess thee with our hymn.

c

3. Laudámus únicum Deum,
   Patrem poténtem, Fílium
   cum Spíritu Paráclito
   in Trinitátis glória.

4. O digne linguis qui piis
   laudéris omni témpore,
   Fili Dei, te sæcula
   uitæ datórem pérsonent.

### 6

*After Benediction. Doxology in the
Evening Prayer of the Apostolic
Constitutions (vii, 48; 4th century)
in Greek; in Latin in St Benedict's
rule (xi; 6th century), to be sung at
the end of Matins*

TE decet laus, te decet hymnus,
tibi glória Deo Patri et Fílio
cum Sancto Spíritu in sæcula
sæculórum. Amen.

3. We praise the one God, almighty Father, Son and Holy Ghost the comforter, in the glory of the Trinity.

4. Son of God, worthy to be glorified at all times by pure tongues, giver of life, all ages proclaim thee.

### 6

*After Benediction. Doxology in the Evening Prayer of the Apostolic Constitutions (vii, 48; 4th century) in Greek; in Latin in St Benedict's rule (xi; 6th century), to be sung at the end of Matins*

TO thee praise, to thee a hymn is due; to thee glory, God the Father and Son with the Holy Ghost, for ever and ever. Amen.

## II. ADVENT HYMNS

### 7

*Vesper hymn in the Breviary (7th cent.)*

CREATOR alme síderum,
 ætérna lux credéntium,
 Iesu redémptor ómnium
inténde uotis súpplicum.

2. Qui dæmonis ne fraúdibus
 períret orbis, ímpetu
 amóris actus lánguidi
 mundi medéla factus es.

3. Commúne qui mundi nefas
 ut expiáres, ad crucem
 e uírginis sacrário
 intácta prodis uíctima.

4. Cuius potéstas glóriæ
 noménque cum primum sonat,
 et cælites et ínferi
 treménte curuántur genu.

5. Te deprecámur últimæ
 magnum diéi iúdicem
 armis supérnæ grátiæ
 defénde nos ab hóstibus.

# II. ADVENT HYMNS

## 7

*Vesper hymn in the Breviary (7th cent.)*

BLESSED Creator of the stars, eternal light of the faithful, Jesus, redeemer of all, hear the prayers of thy servants.

2. Who, lest through frauds of the devil all perish, moved by love becamest the healer of the sick world.

3. To atone for the sin of the world thou camest from the Virgin's womb, a spotless victim, to the cross.

4. Thy glorious power and name when heard make angels and men trembling bend the knee.

5. We pray thee, great judge of the last day, to defend us from our enemies with arms of grace from above.

6. Virtus, honor, laus, glória
Deo Patri cum Fílio,
sanĉto simul Paráclito
in sæculórum sæcula.

8

*Matin hymn in the Breviary (about* 10*th cent.)*

VERBVM supérnum pródiens,
e Patris ætérni sinu,
qui natus orbi súbuenis
labénte cursu témporis:

2. Illúmina nunc péĉtora,
tuóque amóre cóncrema,
ut cor cadúca déserens
cæli uolúptas ímpleat.

3. Vt cum tribúnal iúdicis
damnábit igni nóxios
et uox amíca débitum
uocábit ad cælum pios,

4. Non esca flammárum nigros
uoluámur inter túrbines,
uultu Dei sed cómpotes
cæli fruámur gaúdiis.

5. Patri simúlque Fílio,
tibíque sanĉte Spíritus
sicut fuit sit iúgiter
sæclum per omne glória.

6. Power, honour, praise and glory to God the Father, with the Son and the Holy Comforter, for ever and ever.

## 8

*Matin hymn in the Breviary (about* 10*th cent.*)

HIGH Word of God, coming forth from the eternal Father, who being born in the fullness of time dost succour the world;

2. Enlighten now our hearts and burn them with love of thee, that leaving earthly things they be filled with heavenly joy.

3. And when the tribunal of the great judge condemns the wicked to fire, when his voice calls the good to their reward in heaven,

4. Let us not be cast into the darkness to burn in flames, but may we share the joy of heaven, seeing the face of God.

5. To the Father, to the Son, to the Holy Spirit, as it was, so always for all ages be glory.

9

*The great O's arranged in verse (from a German hymn-book, 1722)*

VENI, ueni Emmánuel,
captíuum solue Israel
qui gemit in exsílio
priuátus Dei Fílio.
Gaude, gaude, Emmánuel
nascétur pro te, Israel.

2. Veni O Iesse uírgula,
ex hostis tuos úngula,
de specu tuos tártari
educ, et antro bárathri.
Gaude, gaude, Emmánuel
nascétur pro te, Israel.

3. Veni, ueni O Oriens,
soláre nos aduéniens,
noctis depélle nébulas
dirásque noctis ténebras.
Gaude, gaude, Emmánuel
nascétur pro te, Israel.

4. Veni Clauis davídica,
regna reclúde cælica,
fac iter tutum súperum
et claude uias ínferum.

## 9

*The great O's arranged in verse (from a
German hymn-book, 1722)*

O COME, O come, Emmanuel,
And ransom captive Israel,
That mourns in lonely exile here
Until the Son of God appear.
Rejoice, rejoice, Emmanuel
Shall come to thee, O Israel.

2. O come, thou Rod of Jesse, free
Thine own from Satan's tyranny,
From depths of hell thy people save
And give them victory o'er the grave.
Rejoice, rejoice, Emmanuel
Shall come to thee, O Israel.

3. O come, thou Day-spring, come and cheer
Our spirits by thine advent here;
Disperse the gloomy clouds of night
And death's dark shadows put to flight.
Rejoice, rejoice, Emmanuel
Shall come to thee, O Israel.

4. O come, thou Key of David, come,
And open wide our heavenly home;
Make safe the way that leads on high
And close the path to misery.

D

Gaude, gaude, Emmánuel
nascétur pro te, Israel.

5. Veni, ueni Adonai,
qui pópulo in Sínai
legem dedísti uértice
in maiestáte glóriæ.
Gaude, gaude, Emmánuel
nascétur pro te, Israel.

# III. CHRISTMAS AND EPIPHANY

## 10

*Hymn in the Breviary for Vespers and Matins*
*(about the 6th century)*

IESV redémptor ómnium
quem lucis ante oríginem
parem patérnæ glóriæ
Pater suprémus édidit.

2. Tu lumen et splendor Patris,
tu spes perénnis ómnium,
inténde quas fundunt preces
tui per orbem séruuli.

Rejoice, rejoice, Emmanuel
Shall come to thee, O Israel.

5. O come, O come, thou Lord of Might,
Who to thy tribes on Sinai's height
In ancient times didst give the law
In cloud and majesty and awe.
Rejoice, rejoice, Emmanuel
Shall come to thee, O Israel.

## III. CHRISTMAS AND EPIPHANY

### 10

*Hymn in the Breviary for Vespers and Matins
(about the 6th century)*

JESUS, Redeemer of all, born of
the high Father before light was
made, equal to him in glory.

2. Thou light and splendour of the
Father, eternal hope of all, hear the
prayers thy servants throughout
the world make to thee.

3. Meménto rerum cónditor
nostri quod olim córporis
sacráta ab aluo uírginis
nascéndo formam súmpseris.

4. Testátur hoc præsens dies
currens per anni círculum
quod solus e sinu Patris
mundi salus aduéneris.

5. Hunc astra, tellus, æquóra,
hunc omne quod cælo subest
salútis auctórem nouæ
nouo salútat cántico.

6. Et nos beáta quos sacri
rigáuit unda sánguinis
natális ob diem tui
hymni tribútum sóluimus.

7. Iesu tibi sit glória
qui natus es de uírgine
cum Patre et almo Spíritu
in sémpiterna sæcula.

3. Remember, maker of all things, thou once didst take our form, born in the holy Virgin's womb.

4. This day as it comes each year, bears witness that thou once didst go forth from the Father to be the world's salvation.

5. Thee, author of new redemption, do stars, earth and sea, do all things under heaven with a new song proclaim.

6. And we, whom thy precious blood has washed, on thy birthday bring the homage of our hymns to thee.

7. Jesus, born of the Virgin, glory to thee, with the Father and the Holy Ghost, for all ages.

II

*By Prudentius, the greatest Latin hymn-writer*
*(d. about 405)*

CORDE natus ex Paréntis
ante mundi exórdium
Alpha et O cognominátus,
ipse fons et claúsula
ómnium quæ sunt, fuérunt
quæque post futúra sunt
sæculórum sæculis.

2. O beátus ortus ille
uirgo cum puérpera
édidit nostram salútem
feta sanĉto Spíritu,
et puer redémptor orbis
os sacrátum prótulit
sæculórum sæculis.

3. Psallat altitúdo cæli,
psallant omnes ángeli,
quidquid est uírtutis unquam
psallant in laudem Dei;
nulla linguárum siléscat
uox et omnis cónsonet
sæculórum sæculis.

## 11

*By Prudentius, the greatest Latin hymn-writer*
*(d. about 405)*

BEGOTTEN of the Father's
love before the world was made,
called Alpha and Omega, he
the source and end of all things that
are, that were, that shall be; for ever
and ever.

2. O blessed birth, when the Virgin
conceiving of the Holy Ghost
brought forth our salvation, when
the Child, redeemer of the world,
lifted his sacred head; for ever and
ever.

3. Let the height of heaven sing;
sing all angels; whatever has life,
sing and praise God. No tongue
shall be silent; sing, every voice; for
ever and ever.

4. Te senes et te iuuéntus,
paruulórum te chorus,
turba matrum uirginúmque
símplices puéllulæ
uoce concórdes pudícis
pérstrepent concéntibus
sæculórum sæculis.

12

*Mediæval Carol*

EX Maria uírgine
puer natus hódie,
Deus qui a sæculis
factus fílius hóminis.
Eia, Iesus hódie
natus est de uírgine.

2. Iacet in præsépio
qui descéndit de cælo
moritúrus in cruce
pro peccánte hómine.
Eia, Iesus hódie
natus est de uírgine.

4. Thee old men and young proclaim; choirs of boys, matrons, maidens, children, joining their voices, sing hymns to thee; for ever and ever.

## 12

*Mediæval Carol*

OF Mary the virgin
a child today is born,
who, God for ever,
becomes the son of man.
Lo, Jesus today
is born of the Virgin.

2. He lies in the manger
who came down from heaven
to die on the cross
for sinful man.
Lo, Jesus today
is born of the Virgin.

E

3. Dum pastóres uígilant
turbæ cáelitum cantant;
in excélsis glóriam,
pacem canunt per terram.
Eia, Iesus hódie
natus est de uírgine.

4. In hoc festo nos omnes,
quia Christe natus es,
iubilémus et tibi
laudes cánimus læti.
Eia, Iesus hódie
natus es de uírgine.

## 13

*Epiphany hymn in the Breviary for Vespers,*
*by Sedulius (5th century)*

CRVDELIS Heródes, Deum
regem ueníre quid times?
Non éripit mortália
qui regna dat cæléstia.

2. Ibant magi quam uíderant
stellam sequéntes práeuiam;
lumen requírunt lúmine,
Deum faténtur múnere.

3. While shepherds watch,
   the heavenly army sings;
   it sings: Glory in the highest
   and peace on earth.
   Lo, Jesus today
   is born of the Virgin.

4. On this feast, because
   thou Christ art born,
   we rejoice and sing
   gladly to thee.
   Lo, Jesus today
   is born of the Virgin.

## 13

*Epiphany hymn in the Breviary for Vespers,*
*by Sedulius (5th century)*

CRUEL Herod, why dost thou
fear when the divine king comes?
He will not take away an earthly
kingdom who brings a heavenly one.

2. The wise men go, following the
star which guides them; by its light
they seek the light, by his grace they
confess God.

3. Lauácra puri gúrgitis
cæléstis agnus áttigit,
peccáta quæ non détulit
nos abluéndo sústulit.

4. Nouum genus poténtiae,
aquae rubéscunt hydriae,
uinúmque iussa fúndere
mutáuit unda oríginem.

5. Iesu tibi sit glória
qui apparuísti géntibus,
cum Patre et almo Spíritu
in sempitérna sáecula.

14

*The last Sunday before Septuagesima.
One of the many mediæval hymns
dismissing the Alleluia till Easter*

ALLELVIA dulce carmen
uox perénnis gaúdii,
Allelúia laus suáuis
est choris cæléstibus
quod canunt Dei manéntes
in domo per sáecula.

3. The Lamb of God is washed in baptism of water; so he, himself without sin, cleanses us of sin.

4. A new kind of miracle. The jars of water are rered; the water commanded to become wine changes its nature.

5. Jesus, to thee glory, who hast shown thyself to gentiles, with the Father and Holy Ghost, for all ages.

### 14

*The last Sunday before Septuagesima. One of the many mediæval hymns dismissing the Alleluia till Easter*

ALLELUIA, glad song, word of eternal joy. Alleluia is the praise of heavenly choirs, sung for ever by those who dwell in the house of God.

2. Allelúia laeta mater
   cóncinis Ierúsalem,
   Allelúia uox tuórum
   ciuium gaudéntium,
   éxsules nos flere cogunt
   Babylónis flúmina.

3. Allelúia non merémur
   nunc perénne psállere,
   Allelúia nos reátus
   cogit interímere;
   tempus instat quo perácta
   lugeámus crímina.

4. Vnde laudándo precámur
   te beáta Trínitas,
   ut tuum nobis uidére
   pascha des in áethere
   quo tibi laeti canámus
   Allelúia pérpetim.

2. Jerusalem, happy mother, thou singest Alleluia. Alleluia is the word of thy joyful citizens. But the waters of Babylon make us exiles rather weep.

3. We are not worthy here always to sing Alleluia. Our sins compel us to interrupt our Alleluia. Now comes the time when we must mourn our past crimes.

4. Wherefore, holy Trinity, praising thee we pray thee to let us see thine Easter on high, in which joyfully forever we may sing to thee Alleluia.

# IV. LENTEN HYMNS

## 15
### *After Benediction*
*Joel* II, 17, *and Ps.* LXXXIV, 6

PARCE Dómine, parce
pópulo tuo: ne in ætér-
num irascáris nobis. (III.)

## 16
### *Vesper hymn in the Breviary*
*(before the* 10*th century)*

AVDI benígne Cónditor
nostras preces cum flétibus
in hoc sacro ieiúnio
fusas quadragenário.

2. Scrútator alme córdium
infírma tu scis uírium,
ad te reuérsis éxhibe
remissiónis grátiam.

## IV. LENTEN HYMNS

### 15

*After Benediction*
*Joel* ii, 17, *and Ps.* LXXXIV, 6

SPARE, O Lord, spare thy people; and be not angry with us for ever. (THRICE.)

### 16

*Vesper hymn in the Breviary*
*(before the* 10*th century)*

HEAR, merciful Creator, the prayers which we make with tears in this holy Lenten fast.

2. Reader of hearts, thou knowest how weak is our strength; show mercy to us who turn to thee.

F

3. Multum quidem peccáuimus
sed parce confiténtibus;
ad nóminis laudem tui
confer medélam lánguidis.

4. Concéde nostrum cónteri
corpus per abstinéntiam
culpæ ut relínquant pábulum
ieiúna corda críminum.

5. Præsta beáta Trínitas,
concéde simplex únitas,
ut fruétuósa sint tuis
ieiuniórum múnera.

17

*Based on Dan. ix, 19, Bar. ii, 16, etc.*

ATTENDE Dómine, et mi-
serére, quia peccáuimus
tibi.
R. Atténde Dómine, et miserére,
quia peccáuimus tibi.

Cantors: 1. Ad te rex summe, ómnium redémptor, óculos nostros
subleuámus flentes; exáudi Christe
supplicántum preces.

3. Much have we sinned, but spare us repentant. For the glory of thy name heal our sick souls.

4. Let our bodies be subdued by abstinence; so may our souls, fasting from all evil, leave the food of sin.

5. Grant, blessed Trinity, divine Unity, that the offerings of our fast be fruitful.

## 17

*Based on Dan. ix, 19, Bar. ii, 16, etc.*

LOOK down, O Lord, and have mercy, for we have sinned against thee.

R. Look down, O Lord, and have mercy, for we have sinned against thee.

Cantors: 1. To thee, high king, Redeemer of all, weeping we lift our eyes; hear Christ the prayers of thy servants.

R. after each verse: Atténde Dómine, et miserére, quia peccáuimus tibi.

2. Déxtera Patris, lapis anguláris, uia salútis, iánua cæléstis, áblue nostri máculas delícti.

3. Rogámus Deus tuam maiestátem, áuribus sacris gémitus exáudi, crímina nostra plácidus indúlge.

4. Tibi fatémur crímina admíssa, contríto corde pándimus occúlta; tua Redémptor píetas ignóscat.

5. Innocens captus nec repúgnans ductus, téstibus falsis pro ímpiis damnátus; quos redemísti tu consérua Christe.

R. after each verse: Look down, O Lord, and have mercy, for we have sinned against thee.

2. Right hand of the Father, cornerstone, path of salvation and gate of heaven, cleanse the stain of our sins.

3. O God, we pray thy majesty, lend thy holy ears to our sighs, mercifully forgive our offences.

4. To thee we confess committed sin, with contrite heart we unveil hidden faults; may thy mercy, Redeemer, forgive.

5. Seized though innocent, led away unresisting, condemned by false witness in place of the guilty, Christ keep those whom thou hast saved.

18

*The hymn of the Cross, by Venan-
tius Fortunatus, Bishop of Poitiers
(d. about 600); sung at Vespers in
Passion-tide and at the procession
on Good Friday morning*

VEXILLA regis pródeunt,
fulget crucis mystérium
qua uita mortem pértulit
et morte uitam prótulit.

2. Quæ uulneráta lánceæ
mucróne diro, críminum
ut nos lauáret sórdibus
manáuit unda et sánguine.

3. Impléta sunt quæ cóncinit
Dauid fidéli cármine
dicéndo natiónibus:
Regnáuit a ligno Deus.

4. Arbor decóra et fúlgida,
ornáta regis púrpura,
elécta digno stípite
tam sancta membra tángere.

## 18

*The hymn of the Cross, by Venantius Fortunatus, Bishop of Poitiers (d. about 600); sung at Vespers in Passion-tide and at the procession on Good Friday morning*

THE banners of the King go forth, the mystery of the cross shines, by which our Life bore death and by death gave us life.

2. To wash us from the stain of sin he was pierced by the sharp point of the lance and shed water and blood.

3. What David in his true hymn told to the nations is now fulfilled: God reigns from the tree.

4. Fair and radiant tree, with royal purple adorned, chosen to touch so sacred limbs with thy boughs.

5. Beáta cuius bráchiis
   prétium pepéndit sæculi,
   statéra faǎta córporis
   tulítque prædam tártari.

6. O crux aue spes única,
   hoc passiónis témpore
   piis adauge grátiam
   reísque dele crímina.

7. Te fons salútis Trínitas
   colláudet omnis spíritus;
   quibus crucis uiǎtóriam
   largíris, adde præmium.

19

*Hymn at Matins in Passion-tide,*
*by Venantius Fortunatus*

PANGE lingua gloriósi
láuream certáminis,
et super crucis trophæo
dic triúmphum nóbilem,
quáliter redémptor orbis
immolátus uícerit.

5. Blessed cross, on whose arms the redemption of the world is borne; thou, from whom his body hangs, dost snatch from hell its prey.

6. O cross hail, our only hope! At this passion-tide increase grace to the good and take sin from the wicked.

7. Thee, holy Trinity fount of salvation, let every spirit praise. To whom thou givest the victory of the cross, to them give also its prize.

## 19

*Hymn at Matins in Passion-tide,*
*by Venantius Fortunatus*

SING, my tongue, the victory of the glorious battle, sing the triumph of the cross; how the Redeemer of the world being sacrificed yet conquered.

2. De paréntis protoplásti
   fraude factor cóndolens,
   quando pomi noxiális
   in necem morsu ruit,
   ipse lignum tunc notáuit
   damna ligni ut sólueret.

3. Hoc opus nostræ salútis
   ordo depopóscerat,
   multifórmis proditóris
   ars ut artem fálleret,
   et medélam ferret inde
   hostis unde læserat.

4. Quando uenit ergo sacri
   plenitúdo témporis,
   missus est ab arce Patris
   natus orbis cónditor,
   atque uentre uirgináli
   carne amíctus pródiit.

5. Vagit infans inter arta
   cónditus præsépia,
   membra pannis inuolúta
   uirgo mater álligat,
   et Dei manus pedésque
   stricta cingit fáscia.

2. The Creator, pitying Adam's race, when it fell by the taste of the forbidden fruit, then noted the tree; that by a tree the loss from a tree should be repaired.

3. So was the work of our salvation ordered, that art should destroy the art of the deceiver, that healing should come from a tree, as had come the wound.

4. Therefore in the fulness of the sacred time the Creator of the world, sent from the Father's home, was born and came forth clothed in flesh from the Virgin's womb.

5. A child he lay in the narrow cradle and the virgin mother bound his limbs in swaddling clothes; such bands held the hands and feet of God.

6. Sempitérna sit beátæ
   Trinitáti glória
   æqua Patri Filióque,
   par decus Paráclito;
   uníus triníque nomen
   laudet uniuérsitas.


## V. EASTERTIDE

### 20

*The Easter Sequence, by Wipo (d. 1048),*
*chaplain to the Emperor Conrad II*

VICTIMAE pascháli laudes
   ímmolent Christiáni.

2. Agnus redémit oves,
   Christus ínnocens Patri
   reconciliáuit peccatóres.

3. Mors et uita duéllo
   conflixére mirándo,
   dux uitæ mórtuus
   regnat uiuus.

6. Eternal glory be to the blessed Trinity, to the Father and Son; the same honour to the Paraclete. Let all the world praise the name of the one and three.

## V. EASTERTIDE

### 20

*The Easter Sequence, by Wipo (d. 1048), chaplain to the Emperor Conrad II*

SING to Christ your paschal victim, Christians sing your Easter hymn.

2. The sinless Lord for sinners,
Christ God's Son for creatures died,
The sheep who strayed, the Lamb of God redeemed.

3. Then death and life their battle
Wonderfully fought, and now
The King of life, once dead, for ever lives.

4. Dic nobis María
quíd uidísti in uia?
Sepúlcrum Christi uiuéntis
et glóriam uidi resurgéntis.

5. Angélicos testes,
sudárium et uestes.
Surréxit Christus spes mea,
præcédet uos in Galiláeam.

6. Scimus Christum surrexísse
a mórtuis uere.
Tu nobis uictor rex miserére.

21

*Vesper hymn in Eastertide (early*
*9th century, considerably modified*
*by the revisers of Urban VIII)*

AD régias agni dapes
stolis amícti cándidis
post tránsitum maris rubri
Christo canámus príncipi;

2. Diuína cuius cáritas
sacrum propínat sánguinem,
almíque membra córporis
amor sacérdos ímmolat.

4. Tell us, Mary, we pray,
   What you saw on Easter day?
   Empty was the grave, and looking
   I saw there the glory of his rising.

5. The angel witnesses
   I saw, and folded linen.
   Christ my hope is risen truly,
   In Galilee he goes before you.

6. We know he rose from death indeed,
   And so to him we pray,
   Great King and Lord of life, bless us
   this day.

21

*Vesper hymn in Eastertide (early
9th century, considerably modified
by the revisers of Urban VIII)*

CALLED to the Lamb's royal
banquet, clothed in white robes,
after crossing the Red sea, let us
sing to Christ the Prince;

2. Whose divine love gives us his
sacred blood; he our high Priest
offers his sacred body.

3. Sparsum cruórem póstibus
uastátor horret ángelus,
fugítque diuísum mare,
mergúntur hostes flúctibus.

4. Iam pascha nostrum Christus est,
paschális idem uíctima
et pura puris méntibus
sinceritátis ázyma.

5. O uera cæli uíctima
subiécta cui sunt tártara,
solúta mortis uíncula,
recépta uitæ præmia.

6. Victor subáctis ínferis
trophæa Christus éxplicat,
cælóque apérto súbditum
regem tenebrárum trahit.

7. Vt sis perénne méntibus
paschále Iesu gáudium,
a morte dira críminum
uitæ renátos líbera.

8. Deo Patri sit glória
et Fílio qui a mórtuis
surréxit ac Paráclito
in sempitérna sæcula.

3. The avenging angel spares the doors marked with blood; the sea dividing turns back, the enemy is plunged in its waves.

4. Now is Christ our Passover; he our paschal sacrifice, pure unleavened bread of sincerity to pure minds.

5. O true heavenly sacrifice by which hell is defeated, the chains of death are broken, the reward of life is obtained.

6. Christ conquering unfolds his standard; hell is driven back and heaven opened, while he overcomes the king of darkness.

7. That thou, Jesu, be the eternal Easter joy of our hearts, set us free from the dread death of sin, who hast given us new life.

8. To God the Father be glory, to the Son who rose from the dead, to the Holy Ghost for eternal ages.

H

22

*Vesper hymn for Ascension Day*
*(about the 5th century)*

SALVTIS humánæ Sator,
Iesu uolúptas córdium,
orbis redémpti cónditor
et casta lux amántium;

2. Qua uictus es cleméntia
ut nostra ferres crímina,
mortem subíres ínnocens
a morte nos ut tólleres.

3. Perrúmpis infernum chaos,
uinctis caténas détrahis,
uictor triúmpho nóbili
ad déxteram Patris sedes.

4. Te cogat indulgéntia
ut damna nostra sárcias,
tuique uultus cómpotes
dites beáto lúmine.

5. Tu dux ad astra et sémita,
sis meta nostris córdibus,
sis lacrymárum gáudium,
sis dulce uitæ præmium.

## 22

*Vesper hymn for Ascension Day*
*(about the 5th century)*

AUTHOR of man's salvation, Jesus, joy of hearts, maker of a world redeemed, pure light of them who love thee;

2. What pity moves thee to bear our sins, that thou guiltless shouldst bear death to save us from death!

3. Thou dost break through the darkness of hell, taking away chains from prisoners; thou conquering in glorious triumph dost sit at the Father's right hand.

4. Let pity move thee to heal our woes, to grant us to see thy face in the blessed light.

5. Leader to heaven and way of life, be thou the end of our desire, thou our joy after tears, thou the reward of life for ever.

# VI. WHITSUNTIDE

## 23

*Vesper hymn for Whitsunday, by*
*Rabanus Maurus, Archbishop of*
*Mainz (d. 856)*

VENI creátor Spíritus,
mentes tuórum uísita,
imple supérna grátia
quæ tu creásti péctora.

2. Qui díceris paráclitus,
altíssimi donum Dei,
fons uiuus, ignis, cáritas
et spiritális únctio.

3. Tu septifórmis múnere,
dígitus patérnæ déxteræ,
tu rite promíssum Patris
sermóne ditans gúttura.

4. Accénde lumen sénsibus,
infúnde amórem córdibus,
infírma nostri córporís
uírtute firmans pérpeti.

# VI. WHITSUNTIDE

## 23

*Vesper hymn for Whitsunday, by Rabanus Maurus, Archbishop of Mainz (d. 856)*

COME Creator Spirit, visit the souls of thy people, fill with grace from on high the hearts which thou hast created.

2. Thou who art called the Comforter, gift of the most high God, living fount, fire, love and unction of souls.

3. Sevenfold in thy gifts, finger of the Father's right hand, thou promised truly by the Father, giving speech to tongues.

4. Inflame our senses with thy light, pour thy love into our hearts, strengthen our weak bodies with lasting power.

5. Hostem repéllas lóngius,
   pacémque dones prótinus;
   ductóre sic te præuio
   uitémus omne nóxium.

6. Per te sciámus da Patrem,
   noscámus atque Fílium,
   teque utriúsque Spíritum,
   credámus omni témpore.

7. Deo Patri sit glória,
   et Fílio qui a mórtuis
   surréxit, ac Paráclito
   in sæculórum sæcula.

## 24

*Sequence of Whitsunday, attributed*
*to King Robert the Pious of France*
*(d. 1031)*

VENI sancte Spíritus,
   et emítte cælitus
   lucis tuæ rádium.

2. Veni pater páuperum,
   ueni dator múnerum,
   ueni lumen córdium.

5. Drive far away the enemy, grant peace at all times; so under thy guidance may we avoid all evil.

6. Grant us by thee to know the Father and to know the Son; and thee, Spirit of both, may we always believe.

7. To God the Father be glory, to the Son who rose from the dead and to the Comforter, for all ages.

## 24

*Sequence of Whitsunday, attributed to King Robert the Pious of France (d. 1031)*

COME Holy Ghost, and send down from heaven the ray of thy light.

2. Come father of the poor, come giver of gifts, come light of hearts.

3. Consolátor óptime,
   dulcis hospes ánimæ,
   dulce refrigérium.

4. In labóre réquies,
   in æstu tempéries,
   in fletu solátium.

5. O lux beatíssima,
   reple cordis íntima
   tuórum fidélium.

6. Sine tuo númine
   nihil est in hómine,
   nihil est innóxium.

7. Laua quod est sórdidum,
   riga quod est áridum,
   sana quod est sáucium.

8. Fleéte quod est rígidum,
   foue quod est frígidum,
   rege quod est déuium.

9. Da tuis fidélibus
   in te confiténtibus
   sacrum septenárium.

10. Da uirtútis méritum,
    da salútis éxitum,
    da perénne gáudium.

3. Best comforter, sweet guest of the soul, sweet refreshment.

4. Rest in labour, shade in the heat, comfort in sorrow.

5. O most blessed light, fill the depth of the hearts of thy faithful.

6. Without thy grace there is nothing in man, nothing not harmful.

7. Cleanse what is unclean, water what is dry, heal what is sick.

8. Bend what is hard, warm what is cold, straighten what is crooked.

9. Give to the faithful who trust in thee thy holy sevenfold gift.

10. Give reward of merit, give salvation at last, give eternal joy.

I

25

*A modern hymn to the Holy Trinity*
*(from J. Mohr: Cantiones Sacræ,*
*Pustet, 1891)*

LAUS tibi Deus Pater tuóque Filio
    qui factus noster frater in hoc exsílio.
Procédit ex utróque sanctus Paráclitus
cum Patre Filióque Deus et dóminus.
Kyrie eléison.

2. Per uincla unitátis coniúnge ánimos,
    nexúsque caritátis tu pange íntimos.
Ne te ad ultiónem delícta próuocent;
dona remissiónem dum nobis dísplicent.
Kyrie eléison.

3. Da ut digne fruámur sacro uiático;
    hoc scuto muniámur in uitæ término,
lætíque sociémur in cæli cúria,
in cælo contemplémur tua mystéria.
Kyrie eléison.

## 25

*A modern hymn to the Holy Trinity
(from J. Mohr: Cantiones Sacræ,
Pustet, 1891)*

PRAISE to thee, God the Father,
and to thy Son who became our
brother in this exile. From both
proceeds the holy Comforter, together with the Father and the Son
God and Lord. Lord have mercy.

2. Join all souls in the bond of union
and fasten close the ties of love. Let
not our sins provoke thee to ven-
geance, but grant forgiveness while
we repent of them. Lord have mercy.

3. Grant that we may receive worthily the holy viaticum, that we may be
defended by this shield at the end
of life. Grant that we be joined in joy
to thy heavenly court, there to see
thy mysteries. Lord have mercy.

## VII. THE HOLY EUCHARIST

### 26

*Antiphon of the Magnificat at the second Vespers of Corpus Christi, by St. Thomas Aquinas (d. 1274)*

O SACRVM conuíuium, in quo Christus súmitur, recólitur memória passiónis eius, mens implétur grátia, et futúræ glóriæ nobis pignus datur. Allelúia.

### 27

*Responsory from the Roman Office*

HOMO quidam fecit cœnam magnam, et misit seruum suum hora cœnæ dícere inuitátis ut uenírent;
Quia paráta sunt ómnia.
V. Veníte comédite panem meum, et bíbite uinum quod míscui uobis;
Quia paráta sunt ómnia.
Glória Patri et Fílio et Spirítui sancto.
Quia paráta sunt ómnia.

# VII. THE HOLY EUCHARIST

## 26

*Antiphon of the Magnificat at the second Vespers of Corpus Christi, by St. Thomas Aquinas (d. 1274)*

O SACRED banquet in which Christ is received, the memory of his passion kept, the soul filled with grace and a pledge of future glory given to us. Alleluia.

## 27

*Responsory from the Roman Office*

A CERTAIN man made a great supper and sent his servant at the hour of supper to tell the invited to come;
For all things are ready.
V. Come, eat my bread and drink the wine I have mixed for you;
For all things are ready.
Glory be to the Father and to the Son and to the Holy Ghost.
For all things are ready.

## 28

*Responsory of the Monastic Office at
Matins for Corpus Christi*

VNVS panis et unum corpus
multi sumus,
Omnes qui de uno pane et de
uno cálice participámus.
V. Parásti in dulcédine tua páuperi
Deus, qui habitáre facis unánimes in
domo.
Omnes qui de uno pane et de uno
cálice participámus.
Glória Patri et Fílio et Spirítui
sancto.
Omnes qui de uno pane et de uno
cálice participámus.

## 29

*Matins hymn for Corpus Christi, by
St. Thomas Aquinas*

SACRIS solémniis iuncta sint gáudia,
et ex præcórdiis sonent præcónia;
recédant uétera, noua sint ómnia,
corda, uoces et ópera.

28

*Responsory of the Monastic Office at
Matins for Corpus Christi*

WE being many are one bread
and one body,
All who share the one bread
and one cup.
V. Thou hast prepared of thy sweetness for the poor, O God, who makest
us to dwell in one mind in thy house.
All who share the one bread and one
cup.
Glory be to the Father and to the
Son and to the Holy Ghost.
All who share the one bread and one
cup.

29

*Matins hymn for Corpus Christi, by
St. Thomas Aquinas*

TO the sacred feast let joy be
joined; praise shall sound from
our hearts; let the old things depart and all be made new, our hearts,
words and deeds.

2. Noctis recólitur cœna nouíssima
   qua Christus créditur agnum et ázyma
   dedísse frátribus iuxta legítima
   priscis indúlta pátribus.

3. Post agnum typicum explétis épulis
   corpus domínicum datum discípulis
   sic totum ómnibus quod totum síngulis
   eius fatémur mánibus.

4. Dedit fragílibus córporis férculum,
   dedit et tristibus sánguinis póculum
   dicens: Accípite quod trado uásculum,
   omnes ex eo bíbite.

5. Sic sacrifícium istud instítuit
   cuius officium commítti uóluit
   solis presbyteris quibus sic cóngruit
   ut sumant et dent cæteris.

6. Panis angélicus fit panis hóminum,
   dat panis cælicus figúris términum.
   O res mirábilis, mandúcat Dóminum
   pauper seruus et húmilis.

7. Te, trina Déitas únaque, póscimus,
   sic tu nos uísita sicut te cólimus.
   Per tuas sémitas duc nos quo téndimus
   ad lucem quam inhábitas.

2. Now we remember the supper of that last evening, in which we know that Christ gave the paschal lamb and the unleavened bread to the brethren, according to the law of the ancient fathers.

3. After the symbol of the lamb, supper being over, we believe that the body of the Lord was given to the disciples by his own hands, whole to all and whole to each one.

4. To the weak he gave his strengthening body, to the sad the cup of his blood, saying: Receive what I give you, drink ye all of it.

5. So he founded this sacrifice, which he committed to priests alone, that they should partake and give to the others.

6. The bread of angels becomes bread of men; the heavenly food makes an end of symbols. O wonderful thing, a poor and lowly servant eats the body of the Lord.

7. We pray thee, Godhead three and one, come to us as we worship thee; lead us by thy path to the goal for which we hope, to the light in which thou dwellest.

K

30

*The last four verses of Lauda Sion,*
*the Sequence for Corpus Christi, by*
*St. Thomas Aquinas*

ECCE panis angelórum
factus cibus uiatórum,
uere panis filiórum
non mitténdus cánibus.

2. In figúris præsignátur
cum Isaac immolátur,
agnus paschæ deputátur,
datur manna pátribus.

3. Bone pastor, panis uere,
Iesu nostri miserére;
tu nos pasce, nos tuére,
tu nos bona fac uidére
in terra uiuéntium.

4. Tu qui cuncta scis et uales,
qui nos pascis hic mortáles,
tuos ibi commensáles,
cohærédes et sodáles,
fac sanctórum cíuium.

30

*The last four verses of Lauda Sion, the Sequence for Corpus Christi, by St. Thomas Aquinas*

BEHOLD the bread of angels made food for pilgrims, true children's bread, not to be given to dogs. (Matt. xv, 26.)

2. This was foretold in types when Isaac was to be sacrificed, when the paschal lamb was chosen and manna was given to the fathers.

3. Good Shepherd and true bread, Jesu have mercy on us. Do thou feed us and keep us, do thou make us to see thy good things in the land of the living.

4. Thou who knowest and canst do all things, who dost feed us here as mortals, give us there to eat of thy table, make us thy heirs and comrades of the citizens of heaven.

31

*Hymn to the Blessed Sacrament,
used in Germany as a Sequence since
the 13th century (Daniel: Thesaurus
hymnol. v, 74)*

O PANIS dulcíssime,
O fidélis ánimæ
uitális reféctio.

2. O paschális uíctimæ,
agne mansuetíssime,
legális oblátio.

3. Caro carens cárie,
quæ sub panis spécie
ueláris diuínitus.

4. Victu multifárie
récrea nos grátiæ
septifórmis Spíritus.

5. Suméntem cum súmeris,
quia non consúmeris
ætérne uiuíficas.

6. Nam reátum scéleris
dono tanti múneris
cleménter puríficas.

### 31

*Hymn to the Blessed Sacrament,
used in Germany as a Sequence since
the 13th century (Daniel: Thesaurus
hymnol. v, 74)*

O MOST sweet bread, life-giving
food of faithful souls.

2. O meek Lamb, lawful offering of
the paschal sacrifice.

3. Immortal flesh veiled by God
under the form of bread.

4. Strengthen us in every way by
the food of grace sevenfold from the
Holy Spirit.

5. When thou art received, not con-
sumed, thou dost give life eternal to
him who receives thee.

6. For by so great a gift thou dost
cleanse mercifully the stain of sin.

7. In te nos ut únias,
   et uirtúte múnias,
   da te digne súmere.

8. Vt carnáles fúrias
   propéllens nos fácias
   tecum pie uiuere.

9. Sic reféčti póculis
   sánguinis et épulis
   tuæ carnis óptimis,

10. Sæculórum sæculis
    epulémur sédulis
    inuitáti ázymis.

## 32

*Communion hymn of the Gallican rite
(in the Bangor antiphonary, 7th
century). The oldest known Latin
Eucharistic hymn*

SANCTI uenite,
   Christi corpus súmite,
   sančtum bibéntes
quo redémpti sánguine.

7. To unite us to thee, to strengthen us in good, grant us to receive thee worthily.

8. Driving away temptation, make us live in holiness with thee.

9. So, comforted by the cup of thy blood, by the holy banquet of thy flesh,

10. For ever and ever we may rejoice, called to the high feast of thy eternal pasch.

### 32

*Communion hymn of the Gallican rite (in the Bangor antiphonary, 7th century). The oldest known Latin Eucharistic hymn*

COME all ye holy,
    take the body of your Lord,
    Drink of his chalice,
take the blood for you outpoured.

2. Saluáti Christi
córpore et sánguine,
a quo reféčti
laudes dicámus Deo.

3. Dator salútis
Christus Fílius Dei
mundum saluáuit
per crucem et sánguinem.

4. Pro uniuérsis
immolátus Dóminus
ipse sacérdos
exístit et hóstia.

5. Lege præcéptum
immolári hóstias
qua adumbrántur
diuína mystéria.

6. Lucis indúltor
et saluátor ómnium
præcláram sančtis
largítus est gratiam.

7. Accédant omnes
pura mente credúli,
sumant ætérnam
salútis custódiam.

2. Saved by his body,
    by his sacred blood, we raise
    Grateful our voices
    unto God in hymns of praise.

3. Giver of life, he
    Christ our Saviour, Son of God,
    Bought our redemption
    by his cross and precious blood.

4. Dying for all men,
    he the Lord prepared this feast,
    Offered as victim,
    offering himself as priest.

5. God to our fathers
    ordered sacrifice of old;
    So he in symbols
    Christ the victim true foretold.

6. Giver of light, the
    one Redeemer of our race,
    He to his holy
    servants gives abundant grace.

7. Come, who with pure hearts
    in the Saviour's word believe;
    Come, and partaking
    saving grace from him receive.

L

8. Sanctórum custos
   rector quoque Dóminus
   uitam perénnem
   largítur credéntibus.

9. Cæléstem panem
   dat esuriéntibus;
   de fonte uiuo
   præbet sitiéntibus.

10. Alpha et Omega
    ipse Christus Dóminus
    uenit uentúrus
    iudicáre hómines.

## 33
*Communion Antiphon of the Gallican
and Milanese rites*

VENITE pópuli ad sacrum et
immortále mystérium et libámen
agéndum; cum timóre et fide ac-
cedámus, mánibus mundis pœnitén-
tiæ munus communicémus; quóniam
Agnus Dei propter nos Patri sacrifícium propósitum est: ipsum solum
adorémus, ipsum glorificémus cum
ángelis clamántes: Allelúia.

8. God our defender,
   guardian sure in this our strife,
   Gives to his faithful
   after death eternal life.

9. He to the hungry
   gives as food this heavenly bread,
   Fountain of life, he
   gives to drink the blood he shed.

10. Christ, source of all things,
    who here feeds us sinful men,
    When his great day dawns,
    judge of all, will come again.

### 33
*Communion Antiphon of the Gallican
and Milanese rites*

COME people, to offer the holy, immortal mystery and sacrifice. Let us approach with fear and faith, to receive the gift of pardon with clean hands. For the Lamb of God for us is offered a sacrifice to his Father. Him alone we adore, him we glorify, crying with the angels: Alleluia.

### 34
*From a 14th cent. Gradual at Limoges*

AVE uerum corpus natum
de María uírgine;
uere passum, immolátum
in cruce pro hómine:
cuius latus perforátum
fluxit aqua et sánguine:
esto nobis prægustátum
mortis in exámine.
O Jesu dulcis, O Jesu pie,
O Jesu fili Maríæ.

### 35
*Hymn by St. Thomas Aquinas*

ADORO te deuóte, latens Déitas,
quæ sub his figúris uere látitas:
tibi se cor meum totum súbicit,
quia te contémplans totum déficit.

2. Visus, tactus, gustus in te fállitur,
sed audítu solo tuto créditur:
credo quidquid dixit Dei Fílius:
nil hoc uerbo ueritátis uérius.

3. In cruce latébat sola Déitas,
at hoc latet simul et humánitas:
ambo tamen credens atque cónfitens,
peto quod petíuit latro pœnitens.

## 34
*From a 14th cent. Gradual at Limoges*

HAIL true Body, born of Mary the virgin; suffering, sacrificed truly on the cross for men; from whose pierced side water flowed and blood. Be merciful to us at the judgement of death, O sweet Jesus, O merciful Jesus, O Jesus Son of Mary.

## 35
*Hymn by St. Thomas Aquinas*

HUMBLY I adore thee, hidden Godhead, veiled truly under these figures. All my heart I give to thee, for it all fails in contemplating thee.

2. Sight, touch and taste tell me nothing of thy presence; yet safely I trust what I hear. I believe whatever the Son of God has said; nothing can be more true than the word of Truth itself.

3. On the cross thy Godhead was hidden; here is hidden thy manhood too. Yet I believe and confess both, praying as prayed the good thief.

4. Plagas, sicut Thomas, non intúeor:
   Deum tamen meum te confíteor:
   fac me tibi semper magis crédere,
   in te spem habére, te dilígere.

5. O memoriále mortis Dómini,
   panis uiuus uitam præstans hómini,
   præsta meæ menti de te uíuere,
   et te illi semper dulce sápere.

6. Pie pellicáne, Iesu Dómine,
   me immúndum munda tuo sánguine,
   cuius una stilla saluum fácere
   totum mundum quit ab omni scélere.

7. Iesu, quem uelátum nunc aspício,
   oro fiat illud quod tam sítio:
   ut te reueláta cernens fácie,
   uisu sim beátus tuæ glóriæ.

## 36
*Hymn at Lauds for Corpus Christi,*
*by St. Thomas Aquinas*

VERBVM supérnum pródiens,
nec Patris linquens déxteram,
   ad opus suum éxiens,
uenit ad uitæ uésperam.

4. I do not see thy wounds like Thomas; yet I confess thee my God. Grant that I may ever more and more believe in thee, hope in thee, love thee.

5. O memory of the death of the Lord, living bread giving life to man, let me ever live of thee, ever sweetly taste thee.

6. Pelican of mercy, Jesus Lord, cleanse me, unclean, by thy blood, of which one drop is enough to wash the world of all sin.

7. Jesus, whom now I see veiled, I pray that this may come for which I long so much, that at last, seeing thee face to face, I may be blessed by the sight of thy glory.

## 36

*Hymn at Lauds for Corpus Christi, by St. Thomas Aquinas*

THE Word most high coming forth, yet not leaving the Father's right hand, having done his work, comes to the evening of his life.

2. In mortem a discípulo
   suis tradéndus æmulis,
   prius in uitæ férculo
   se trádidit discípulis.

3. Quibus sub bina spécie
   carnem dedit et sánguinem,
   ut dúplicis substántiæ
   totum cibáret hóminem.

4. Se nascens dedit sócium,
   conuéscens in edúlium,
   se móriens in prétium,
   se regnans dat in præmium.

O SALVTARIS Hóstia,
   quæ cæli pandis óstium:
   bella premunt hostília,
   da robur, fer auxílium.

6. Vni trinóque Dómino
   sit sempitérna glória,
   qui uitam sine término
   nobis donet in pátria.

2. When the disciple was about to give him over to his enemies for death, first he gave himself as food of life to his disciples;

3. To whom under two kinds he gave his flesh and blood, that he should feed man's twofold nature.

4. When he was born he came to be our friend, at supper he gave himself to be our food, dying he is our ransom, reigning he shall be our reward.

O SAVING Victim, who openest the gate of heaven, war rages round us; give strength, bring help.

6. To the Lord three and one be glory for ever; and may he give us life without end in our home above.

M

## 37

*Hymn at Vespers for Corpus Christi,
by St. Thomas Aquinas*

PANGE lingua gloriósi
  córporis mystérium,
  sanguinísque pretiósi,
quem in mundi prétium
fructus ventris generósi
rex effúdit géntium.

2. Nobis datus, nobis natus
  ex intácta uírgine,
  et in mundo conuersátus
  sparso uerbi sémine,
  sui moras incolátus
  miro clausit órdine.

3. In suprémæ nocte cœnæ
  recúmbens cum frátribus,
  obseruáta lege plene
  cibis in legálibus,
  cibum turbæ duodénæ
  se dat suis mánibus.

4. Verbum caro, panem uerum
  uerbo carnem éfficit:
  fitque sanguis Christi merum,
  et si sensus déficit,
  ad firmándum cor sincérum
  sola fides súfficit.

## 37

*Hymn at Vespers for Corpus Christi,
by St. Thomas Aquinas*

SING, my tongue, the mystery of the glorious body and of the precious blood, which, fruit of the blessed womb, he the King of nations gave to ransom the world.

2. Given to us, born for us of a spotless virgin, he dwelt on earth, sowing the seed of his word, till with a wonderful rite he closed his life.

3. In the night of the last supper, seated with the brethren, having fulfilled all the law required, to the twelve with his own hands as food he gives himself.

4. Word made flesh, by his word he changes bread into his body and wine becomes the blood of Christ. If our senses fail us, faith alone will make a true heart firm.

TANTVM ergo sacraméntum
uenerémur cérnui,
et antíquum documéntum
nouo cedat rítui;
præstet fides suppleméntum
sénsuum deféctui.

6. Genitóri, genitóque
laus et jubilátio,
salus honor uirtus quoque
sit et benedíctio;
procedénti ab utróque
compar sit laudátio.

At Benediction the following prayer is here
said:

V. Panem de cælo præstitísti eis. (AT EASTER-
TIDE: Allelúia.)

R. Omne delectaméntum in se habéntem. (AT
EASTERTIDE: Allelúia.)

Orémus.

DEVS, qui nobis sub sacraménto mirábili
passiónis tuæ memóriam reliquísti, tríbue quæsumus, ita nos córporis et sánguinis tui sacra mystéria uenerári; ut redémpt-
iónis tuæ fructum in nobis iúgiter sentiámus.
Qui uiuis et regnas in sæcula sæculórum. Amen.

BOWING low then let us worship so great a Sacrament. The old law gives place to a new rite, faith supplies the lack of sight.

6. To the Father and to the Son be praise and glory, salvation, honour, power and blessing; to him who from both proceeds be the same worship.

At Benediction the following prayer is here said:
V. Thou didst give them bread from heaven. (AT EASTERTIDE: Alleluia.)
R. Containing in itself all sweetness. (AT EASTERTIDE: Alleluia.)
Let us pray.

O GOD, who in this wonderful Sacrament hast left us a remembrance of thy passion, grant us, we beseech thee, so to reverence the sacred mysteries of thy body and blood that we may ever feel within us the fruit of thy redemption. Who livest and reignest, world without end. Amen.

## 38

*Antiphon & Psalm sung after Benediction*

ADOREMUS in ætérnum sanctíssimum sacraméntum.
Ps. cxvi. 1. Laudáte Dóminum omnes gentes: laudáte eum omnes pópuli:
2. Quóniam confirmáta est super nos misericórdia ejus: et uéritas Dómini manet in ætérnum.
Glória Patri et Fílio et Spíritui sancto.
Sicut erat in princípio, et nunc, et semper, et in sæcula sæculórum. Amen.
Adorémus in ætérnum sanctíssimum sacramentum.

## 39

*Response from the Liturgy of the Apostolic Constitutions*, VIII, 13, 13

VNVS sanctus, unus dóminus, Iesus Christus in glória Dei Patris. Benedictus es in sæcula. Amen. Glória in altíssimis Deo et in terra pax, in homínibus bona uolúntas. Hosánna fílio Dauid; benedictus qui uenit in nómine Dómini. Deus dóminus et appáruit nobis. Hosánna in altíssimis.

## 38
*Antiphon & Psalm sung after Benediction*

LET us worship for ever the most holy
Sacrament.
Ps.cxvi.1.Praise the Lord, all ye nations;
praise him, all ye people.
2.Because his mercy is confirmed upon us:and
the truth of the Lord remaineth for ever.
Glory be to the Father and to the Son and to
the Holy Ghost.
As it was in the beginning, is now, and ever
shall be, world without end. Amen.
Let us worship for ever the most holy Sacrament.

## 39
*Response from the Liturgy of the Apostolic
Constitutions, VIII, 13, 13*

ONE is holy, one is Lord, Jesus Christ in
the glory of God the Father. Blessed
art thou for ever. Amen. Glory to God
on high, and on earth peace, good will among
men. Hosanna to the Son of David; blessed
is he who comes in the name of the Lord.
God is Lord and has shown himself to us.
Hosanna in the highest.

# VIII. THE BLESSED VIRGIN MARY

## 40

*Our Lady's own hymn (Luke 1, 46–55)*

MAGNIFICAT* ánima mea Dóminum:
2. Et exsultáuit * spíritus meus in Deo
salutári meo.

3. Quia respéxit humilitátem ancíllæ suæ: *
ecce enim ex hoc beátam me dicent omnes
generatiónes.

4. Quia fecit mihi magna qui potens est: * et
sanctum nomen eius.

5. Et misericórdia eius a progénie in progénies *
timéntibus eum.

6. Fecit poténtiam in bráchio suo: * dispérsit
supérbos mente cordis sui.

7. Depósuit poténtes de sede, * et exaltáuit
húmiles.

8. Esuriéntes impléuit bonis:* et díuites dimísit
inánes.

9. Súscepit Israel púerum suum, * recordátus
misericórdiæ suæ.

10. Sicut locútus est ad patres nostros, * Abraham et sémini eius in sæcula.

11. Glória Patri et Fílio * et Spirítui sancto.

12. Sicut erat in princípio, et nunc et semper *
et in sæcula sæculórum. Amen.

## VIII. THE BLESSED VIRGIN MARY

### 40

*Our Lady's own hymn (Luke i, 46–55)*

MY SOUL doth magnify the Lord:
2. And my spirit hath rejoiced in God
my Saviour.

3. Because he hath regarded the lowliness of his handmaid; for behold from henceforth all generations shall call me blessed.

4. Because he that is mighty hath done great things to me: and holy is his name.

5. And his mercy is from generation unto generation to them that fear him.

6. He hath showed might in his arm: he hath scattered the proud in the conceit of their heart.

7. He hath put down the mighty from their seat, and hath exalted the humble.

8. He hath filled the hungry with good things: and the rich he hath sent empty away.

9. He hath received Israel his servant, being mindful of his mercy.

10. As he spoke to our fathers, to Abraham and to his seed for ever.

11. Glory be to the Father and to the Son and to the Holy Ghost.

12. As it was in the beginning, is now and ever shall be, world without end. Amen.

N

41

*Hymn at Vespers on feasts of the*
*Blessed Virgin (7th century)*

AVE maris stella,
   Dei mater alma,
   atque semper uirgo,
felix cæli porta.

2. Sumens illud Aue
   Gabriélis ore,
   funda nos in pace,
   mutans Euæ nomen.

3. Solue uincla reis,
   profer lumen cæcis,
   mala nostra pelle,
   bona cuncta posce.

4. Monstra te esse matrem,
   sumat per te preces,
   qui pro nobis natus
   tulit esse tuus.

5. Virgo singuláris,
   inter omnes mitis,
   nos culpis solútos
   mites fac et castos.

## 41

*Hymn at Vespers on feasts of the Blessed Virgin (7th century)*

HAIL star of the sea, blessed mother of God and ever virgin, happy gate of heaven.

2. Receiving that Ave from the mouth of Gabriel establish us in peace, changing the name of Eve (Eva).

3. Loosen the chains of sinners, give light to the blind, drive away our ills, obtain for us all good things.

4. Show thyself a mother; may he hear thy prayers who, born for us, was willing to be thy Son.

5. Virgin above all others, meeker than all, make us free from sin, meek and pure.

6. Vitam præsta puram,
   iter para tutum,
   ut uidéntes Iesum,
   semper collætémur.

7. Sit laus Deo Patri,
   summo Christo decus,
   Spirítui sancto,
   tribus honor unus.

### 42

*Hymn at Lauds of the Blessed Virgin,
by Venantius Fortunatus (c. 600)*

O GLORIOSA uírginum,
   sublímis inter sídera,
   qui te creáuit, páruulum
lacténte nutris úbere.

2. Quod Eua tristis ábstulit,
   tu reddis almo gérmine:
   intrent ut astra flébiles,
   cæli reclúdis cárdines.

3. Tu regis alti iánua
   et aula lucis fúlgida:
   uitam datam per uírginem
   gentes redémptæ pláudite.

6. Obtain for us a pure life, make safe our path, that seeing Jesus we may ever rejoice with thee.

7. To God the Father be praise, glory to Christ on high, honour to the Holy Ghost, one in three.

### 42

*Hymn at Lauds of the Blessed Virgin, by Venantius Fortunatus (c. 600)*

GLORIOUS among virgins, high above the stars, thou dost nourish at thy breast as a child him who created thee.

2. What unhappy Eve lost thou dost restore by thy holy Child; thou dost open the gates of heaven that sinners may rise to the stars.

3. Thou art queen of the gates on high and of the shining halls of light. People redeemed, praise the life given through the Virgin.

4. Iesu tibi sit glória,
   qui natus es de uírgine,
   cum Patre et almo Spíritu
   in sempitérna sæcula.


### 43
*Hymn in the Little Office of our Lady*
*(based on number 10)*

MEMENTO rerum cónditor,
nostri quod olim córporis,
sacráta ab aluo uírginis
nascéndo, formam súmpseris.

2. María mater grátiæ,
   dulcis parens cleméntiæ,
   tu nos ab hoste prótege,
   et mortis hora súscipe.

3. Iesu tibi sit glória,
   qui natus es de uírgine,
   cum Patre et almo Spíritu
   in sempitérna sæcula.

4. Jesus, to thee be glory who art born of the Virgin, with the Father and the Holy Ghost for ever and ever.

### 43

*Hymn in the Little Office of our Lady*
*(based on number* 10)

REMEMBER, maker of all things, thou once didst take our form, born in the holy Virgin's womb.

2. Mary, mother of grace, dear mother of mercy, defend us against the enemy, welcome us at the hour of death.

3. Jesus, born of the Virgin, glory to thee, with the Father and the Holy Ghost, for all ages.

### 44

*Hymn of the Carmelites*

SALVE mater misericórdiæ,
mater Dei et mater uéniæ,
mater spei et mater grátiæ,
mater plena sanctæ lætítiæ,
O María.
CHOIR:
Salue mater misericórdiæ,
mater Dei et mater uéniæ,
mater spei et mater grátiæ,
mater plena sanctæ lætítiæ,
O María.

1. Salue decus humáni géneris,
salue uirgo dígnior céteris,
quæ uírgines omnes transgréderis,
et áltius sedes in súperis,
O María.
CHOIR: Salue mater, etc.

2. Salue felix uirgo puérpera:
nam qui sedet in Patris déxtera,
cælum regens, terram et æthera,
intra tua se clausit uíscera,
O María.
CHOIR: Salue mater, etc.

### 44
*Hymn of the Carmelites*

HAIL, mother of mercy, mother of God and mother of pity, mother of hope and mother of grace, mother full of holy joy, O Mary.

CHOIR:
Hail, mother of mercy, mother of God and mother of pity, mother of hope and mother of grace, mother full of holy joy, O Mary.

1. Hail, honour of the human race; hail, virgin worthier than all, who dost excel all virgins and sittest higher than all others in heaven, O Mary.
CHOIR: Hail, mother of mercy, etc.

2. Hail, happy virgin and mother. For he who sits at the Father's right hand, ruling heaven, earth and sky, was borne in thy womb, O Mary.
CHOIR: Hail, mother of mercy, etc.

o

3. Te creáuit Pater ingénitus,
   obumbráuit te Vnigénitus,
   fœcundáuit te sanctus Spíritus,
   tu es facta tota diuínitus,
        O María.
   CHOIR: Salue mater, etc.

4. Te creáuit Deus mirábilem,
   te respéxit ancíllam húmilem,
   te quæsíuit sponsam amábilem,
   tibi numquam fecit consímilem,
        O María.
   CHOIR: Salue mater, etc.

5. Te beátam laudáre cúpiunt
   omnes iusti, sed non suffíciunt;
   multas laudes de te concípiunt,
   sed in illis prorsus defíciunt,
        O María.
   CHOIR: Salue mater, etc.

6. Esto Mater nostrum solácium;
   nostrum esto tu Virgo gáudium;
   et nos tandem post hoc exsílium,
   lætos iunge choris cæléstium,
        O María.
   CHOIR: Salue mater, etc.

3. The eternal Father created thee, the only-begotten Son overshadowed thee, of the Holy Ghost thou didst conceive, thou art all made by God, O Mary.

CHOIR: Hail, mother of mercy, etc.

4. God made thee wonderful, he looked upon thee his lowly handmaid, he sought thee to be the mother of his Son; he made no other like thee, O Mary.

CHOIR: Hail, mother of mercy, etc.

5. All good men would call thee blessed, but they cannot praise thee enough; they sing hymns of thee, yet not worthy of thee, O Mary.

CHOIR: Hail, mother of mercy, etc.

6. Mother, be our comfort; Virgin, be our joy; and may we after this exile join thee among the choirs of heaven, O Mary.

CHOIR: Hail, mother of mercy, etc.

## 45
*Prose written about the 11th century*

INVIOLATA, íntegra et casta es María,
quæ es efféɑta fúlgida regis porta.
O mater alma Christi caríssima,
súscipe pia laudum precámina.
Te nunc flágitant deuóta corda et ora,
nostra ut pura péɑtora sint et córpora.
Tua per precáta dulcísona
nobis concédas uéniam per sæcula.
O benígna, O regína, O María,
quæ sola inuioláta permansísti.

## 46
*Sequence for the feast of the Seven Dolours
of the Blessed Virgin, by Jacopone da Todi
(d. 1306)*

STABAT mater dolorósa
iuxta crucem lacrimósa,
dum pendébat fílius.

2. Cuius ánimam geméntem,
contristátam et doléntem,
pertransíuit gládius.

## 45

*Prose written about the 11th century*

INVIOLATE, spotless and pure art thou, O Mary, who wast made the radiant gate of the King. Holy mother of Christ most dear, receive our devout hymn and praise. Our hearts and tongues now ask of thee that our souls and bodies may be pure. By thy holy prayers obtain for us forgiveness for ever. O gracious queen, O Mary, who alone among women art inviolate.

## 46

*Sequence for the feast of the Seven Dolours of the Blessed Virgin, by Jacopone da Todi (d. 1306)*

SORROWFUL, weeping stood the mother by the cross on which hung her Son.

2. Whose soul, mournful, sad, lamenting, was pierced by a sword.

2. O quam tristis et afflícta
fuit illa benedícta
mater Vnigéniti!

4. Quæ mœrébat et dolébat,
pia mater dum uidébat
nati pœnas ínclyti.

5. Quis est homo qui non fleret
matrem Christi si uidéret
in tanto supplício?

6. Quis non posset contristári,
Christi matrem contemplári
doléntem cum fílio?

7. Pro peccátis suæ gentis
uidit Iesum in torméntis,
et flagéllis súbditum.

8. Vidit suum dulcem natum
moriéndo desolátum,
dum emísit spíritum.

9. Eia mater, fons amóris,
me sentíre uim dolóris
fac ut tecum lúgeam.

10. Fac ut árdeat cor meum
in amándo Christum Deum,
ut sibi compláceam.

3. Oh how sad, how afflicted was that blessed mother of the Only-begotten.

4. How did she mourn and lament, loving mother, while she saw the torment of her divine Son.

5. What man would not weep if he saw the mother of Christ in such sorrow?

6. Who would not mourn with her, seeing Christ's mother mourning with her Son?

7. For the sins of his race she sees Jesus scourged and in torment.

8. She sees her dear Son dying in anguish, as he gives up the ghost.

9. O mother, fount of love, make me feel the strength of thy sorrow, that I may mourn with thee.

10. Make my heart burn with love for Christ my God, that I may please him.

11. Sancta mater, istud agas,
crucifíxi fige plagas
cordi meo uálide.

12. Tui nati uulneráti,
tam dignáti pro me pati,
pœnas mecum díuide.

13. Fac me tecum pie flere,
crucifíxo condolére,
donec ego uíxero.

14. Iuxta crucem tecum stare,
et me tibi sociáre
in planctu desídero.

15. Virgo uírginum præclára,
mihi iam non sis amára:
fac me tecum plángere.

16. Fac ut portem Christi mortem,
passiónis fac consórtem,
et plagas recólere.

17. Fac me plagis uulnerári,
fac me cruce inebriári,
et cruóre fílii.

18. Flammis ne urar succénsus,
per te Virgo sim defénsus
in die iudícii.

11. Holy mother, do this: fix the wounds of the Crucified firmly in my heart.

12. Share with me the pain of thy wounded Son, who deigns to bear so much for me.

13. While I live let me mourn with thee, suffering with him who bore the cross.

14. I wish to stand with thee by the cross and to share thy woe.

15. Blessed virgin of all virgins, be not hard to me, let me weep with thee.

16. Let me remember the death of Christ, give me a share in his passion, thinking of his pain.

17. Let me be wounded with his wounds, be filled with the cross and precious blood of thy Son.

18. That I may not burn in flames, may I be protected by thee, holy Virgin, at the day of judgement.

P

19. Christe, cum sit hinc exíre,
    da per matrem me veníre
    ad palmam uictóriæ.

20. Quando corpus moriétur,
    fac ut ánimæ donétur
    Paradísi glória.

## IX. OTHER SAINTS

### 47

*Vesper hymn for St. John the Baptist,*
*by Paul the Deacon, O.S.B. (d. 799)*

VT queant laxis resonáre fibris
mira gestórum fámuli tuórum,
solue pollúti lábii reátum,
Sancte Ioánnes.

2. Núntius celso uéniens Olympo,
   te patri magnum fore nascitúrum,
   nomen et uitæ sériem geréndæ
   órdine promit.

19. Christ, when I leave this world, grant me to come by thy mother to the palm of victory.

20. When the body dies, grant that my soul may enter the glory of paradise.

## IX. OTHER SAINTS

### 47

*Vesper hymn for St. John the Baptist, by Paul the Deacon, O.S.B. (d. 799)*

THAT the servants of God with clear voices may sing the wonders of thy life, obtain forgiveness for unworthy lips, O holy John.

2. A messenger, coming from high heaven, told thy father that thou wouldst be born great; he declared thy name and the manner of thy life in order.

3. Ille promíssi dúbius supérni
   pérdidit promptæ módulos loquélæ:
   sed reformásti génitus perémptæ
   órgana uocis.

4. Ventris obstrúso récubans cubíli,
   sénseras regem thálamo manéntem:
   hinc parens nati méritis utérque
   ábdita pandit.

5. Sit decus Patri, genitæque Proli,
   et tibi compar utriúsque uirtus
   Spíritus semper, Deus unus, omni
   témporis æuo.

### 48

*Vesper hymn for St. Peter & St. Paul,
attributed to the wife of Boethius
(5th century), considerably altered in
1629*

DECORA lux æternitátis áuream
diem beátis irrigáuit ígnibus,
apostolórum quæ corónat príncipes,
reísque in astra líberam pandit uiam.

3. Thy father, doubting the message from on high, lost the gift of speech; but thou when born didst heal the organs of his voice.

4. Hidden before birth thou knewest the coming of the King; so did both mothers through their sons declare secret things.

5. To the Father be praise, to his only-begotten Son and to thee Holy Spirit, equal in might to both, one God for ever.

### 48

*Vesper hymn for St. Peter & St. Paul, attributed to the wife of Boethius (5th century), considerably altered in 1629*

BRIGHT light of eternity with happy radiance shines on the golden day which crowns the princes of the apostles, opening to sinners a clear path to the stars.

2. Mundi magíster atque cæli iánitor,
   Romæ paréntes, arbitríque géntium,
   per ensis ille, hic per crucis uíctor necem
   uitæ senátum laureáti póssident.

3. O Roma felix, quæ duórum príncipum
   es consecráta glorióso sánguine;
   horum cruóre purpuráta céteras
   excéllis orbis una pulchritúdines.

4. Sit Trinitáti sempitérna glória,
   honor, potéstas, atque iubilátio,
   in unitáte quæ gubérnat ómnia,
   per uniuérsa sæculórum sæcula.

### 49
*Vesper hymn for All Saints* (*14th century*)

PLACARE Christe séruulis,
quibus Patris cleméntiam
tuæ ad tribúnal grátiæ
patróna Virgo póstulat.

2. Et uos beáta per nouem
   distíncta gyros ágmina,
   antíqua cum præséntibus
   futúra damna péllite.

2. Teacher of the world and door-keeper of heaven, fathers of Rome and judges of nations (Mat. xix, 28); conquering, the one by death of the sword, the other by the cross, now crowned they sit in the courts of life.

3. O happy Rome, hallowed by the glorious death of the two princes; purpled by their blood thou alone art fairer than all other cities.

4. To the Trinity be eternal glory, honour, power and praise, who in unity rules all things for all ages.

### 49
*Vesper hymn for All Saints* (14*th century*)

HAVE pity, Christ, on thy servants, for whom at thy mercy-seat the Virgin asks the Father's grace.

2. And you, blessed army of heaven ordered in nine choirs, drive away past evils with those present and to come.

3. Apóstoli cum uátibus,
   apud seuérum iúdicem
   ueris reórum flétibus
   expóscite indulgéntiam.

4. Vos purpuráti mártyres,
   uos candidáti præmio
   confessiónis, éxsules
   uocáte nos in pátriam.

5. Choréa casta uírginum,
   et quos erémus íncolas
   transmísit astris, cælitum
   locáte nos in sédibus.

6. Auférte gentem pérfidam
   credéntium de fínibus,
   ut unus omnes únicum
   ouíle nos pastor regat.

7. Deo Patri sit glória,
   natóque Patris único,
   sanĉto simul Paráclito,
   in sempitérna sæcula.

3. Apostles and prophets, pray the great Judge to forgive us, who truly mourn our sins.

4. Ye martyrs purple-stained, and you white-robed in glorious confession of faith, call us exiles to our home.

5. Pure choir of virgins, hermits whom the desert sent to heaven, place us on thrones above.

6. Drive away the treacherous race from the land of the faithful, that one Shepherd may rule us all, one flock.

7. To God the Father be glory, and to the only-begotten Son, with the Holy Ghost for ever and ever.

50
*Hymn for Apostles at Matins,*
*by St. Ambrose (d. 397)*

ÆTERNA Christi múnera,
apostolórum glóriam,
palmas et hymnos débitos
lætis canámus méntibus.

2. Ecclesiárum príncipes,
belli triumpháles duces,
cæléstis aulæ mílites
et uera mundi lúmina.

3. Deuóta sanctórum fides,
inuícta spes credéntium,
perfécta Christi cáritas
mundi tyránnum cónterit.

4. In his patérna glória,
in his triúmphat Fílius,
in his uolúntas Spíritus,
cælum replétur gáudio.

5. Patri simúlque Fílio,
tibíque sancte Spíritus,
sicut fuit, sit iúgiter
sæclum per omne glória.

50
*Hymn for Apostles at Matins,*
*by St. Ambrose (d. 397)*

FOR the eternal gifts of Christ, for the glory of the apostles and their palms, let us sing hymns with joyful minds.

2. These are the princes of the Church, triumphant leaders of war, warriors of the court of heaven, true lights of the world.

3. The true faith of the saints, the unconquered hope of the faithful, the perfect love of Christ overcome the tyrant of the world.

4. In these the glory of the Father and Son triumphs; in these is the will of the Holy Ghost; by them heaven is filled with joy.

5. To the Father, to the Son, to thee, Holy Spirit, as it was, be always glory in every age.

### 51

*Vesper hymn for a Martyr (11th century,*
*from Milan)*

DEVS tuórum mílitum
sors et coróna, præmium,
laudes canéntes mártyris
absólue nexu críminis.

2. Hic nempe mundi gáudia
et blanda fraudum pábula
imbúta felle députans
peruénit ad cæléstia.

3. Pœnas cucúrrit fórtiter,
et sústulit uiríliter,
fundénsque pro te sánguinem
ætérna dona póssidet.

4. Ob hoc precátu súpplici
te póscimus piíssime:
in hoc triúmpho mártyris
dimítte noxam séruulis.

5. Laus et perénnis glória
Patri sit atque Fílio,
sanĉto simul Paráclito,
in sempitérna sæcula.

## 51

*Vesper hymn for a Martyr (11th century, from Milan)*

GOD, of thy soldiers the lot, crown and reward, free from bonds of sin those who sing the martyr's praise.

2. For he, deeming the joys of the world and the tempting pleasures of sin full of bitterness, so came to heaven.

3. Bravely he went to his torment, manfully he bore it; so shedding his blood for thee he now possesses eternal joy.

4. In humble prayer we beg thee, most merciful, on this triumph of the martyr, to wash away thy servants' guilt.

5. Honour and glory for ever be to the Father and to the Son, with the Holy Ghost, for ever and ever.

## 52
*Hymn for a Confessor at Vespers*
(10*th century*)

ISTE conféssor Dómini, coléntes
quem pie laudant pópuli per orbem,
hac die lætus méruit beátas
    scándere sedes.

OR

hac die lætus méruit suprémos
    laudis honóres.

2. Qui pius, prudens, húmilis, pudícus,
sóbriam duxit sine labe uitam,
donec humános animáuit auræ
    spíritus artus.

3. Cuius ob præstans méritum frequénter,
ægra quæ passim iacuére membra,
uíribus morbi dómitis, salúti
    restituúntur.

4. Noster hinc illi chorus obsequéntem
cóncinit laudem, celebrésque palmas;
ut piis eius précibus iuuémur
    omne per æuum.

5. Sit salus illi, decus atque uirtus,
qui super cæli sólio corúscans,
tótius mundi sériem gubérnat
    trinus et unus.

## 52
### *Hymn for a Confessor at Vespers*
### (10*th century*)

THIS confessor of the Lord, whom people throughout the world praise with due honour, on this day deserved to rise happily to the blessed thrones.

OR

on this day deserves joyfully to receive honour of praise.

2. Who faithful, wise, humble, pure, while breath filled his mortal frame led a holy life without blame.

3. For whose great merit, often those who lay sick, conquering the power of disease, were restored to health.

4. So our choir sings his praise, that we may be helped by his prayers at all times.

5. To God, three in one, who shines above the throne of heaven governing the course of all the world, be honour, glory, power.

# X. THE CITY OF GOD

## 53
### *Prayer for Peace, in the Roman Breviary*

DA pacem Dómine in diebus nostris, quia non est álius qui pugnat pro nobis nisi tu Deus noster.

## 54
### *Matt.* XVI, 18, *& Prayer for the Pope (Ps.* XL, 3)

TV es Petrus, et super hanc petram ædificábo ecclésiam meam.
Orémus pro pontífice nostro N.
R. Dóminus conséruet eum, et uiuíficet eum, et beátum fáciat eum in terra, et non tradat eum in ánimam inimicórum eius.

## 55
### *Prayer for the Bishop (at Lauds and Vespers; Mich.* V, 4)

OREMUS pro antístite nostro N.
R. Stet et pascat in fortitúdine tua Dómine, in sublimitáte nóminis tui.

# X. THE CITY OF GOD

## 53
### *Prayer for Peace, in the Roman Breviary*

GIVE peace, O Lord, in our days; for there is no other who fights for us but thou, our God.

## 54
### *Matt.* XVI, 18, *& Prayer for the Pope (Ps.* XL, 3)

THOU art Peter, and upon this rock I will build my Church.
Let us pray for our pontiff N.
R. May the Lord keep him and give him life and bless him on earth, and not deliver him to the will of his enemies.

## 55
### *Prayer for the Bishop (at Lauds and Vespers; Mich.* v, 4)

LET us pray for our bishop N.
R. May he stand and feed his flock in thy power, O Lord, in the majesty of thy name.

R

### 56

*Antiphon sung by St. Augustine of Canterbury
and his monks when they landed in England
(597). cfr Dan.* ix, 16

DEPRECAMVR te Dómine, in omni
misericórdia tua, ut auferátur furor
tuus et ira tua a ciuitáte ista et de domo
sancta tua, quóniam peccáuimus. Allelúia.

### 57

*Vesper hymn for the Dedication of a Church*
(*8th century*)

VRBS Ierusalem beáta,
dicta pacis uísio,
quæ constrúitur in cælis
uiuis ex lapídibus,
et ángelis coronáta,
ut sponsáta cómite.

2. Noua uéniens e cælo,
nuptiáli thálamo
præparáta, ut sponsáta
copulétur Dómino:
platéæ et muri eius
ex auro puríssimo.

## 56

*Antiphon sung by St. Augustine of Canterbury
and his monks when they landed in England
(597). cfr Dan.* ix, 16

WE beseech thee, O Lord, in all thy
mercy, that thy anger and thy wrath
be taken from this city and from thy
holy house, for we have sinned. Alleluia.

## 57

*Vesper hymn for the Dedication of a Church
(8th century)*

BLESSED city Jerusalem, called vision of
peace, built in heaven of living stones,
encircled with angels as a bride with her
maids.

2. Coming down new from heaven, adorned
like a spouse for marriage, let her be wedded
to the Lord. And all her streets and walls gleam
with purest gold.

3. Portæ nitent margarítis
ádytis paténtibus;
et uirtúte meritórum
illuc introdúcitur
omnis qui ob Christi nomen
hic in mundo prémitur.

4. Tunsiónibus, pressúris
expolíti lápides
suis coaptántur locis
per manus artíficis;
disponúntur permansúri
sacris ædifíciis.

5. Glória et honor Deo
usquequáque altíssimo,
una Patri, Filióque,
ínclyto Paráclito,
cui laus est et potéstas
per ætérna sǽcula.

3. Her gates shine with pearls, standing ever open. For his reward each one may enter there, who for Christ's name has suffered here on earth.

4. Her stones, polished by hammer-strokes and sharp blows, are fitted by the Builder's hands, each in its place, to stay firm in the holy house of God.

5. Glory and honour to God most high in every place; the same glory to Father, Son and Holy Ghost, to whom be praise and power for ever and ever.

58

*Sequence for the Dedication of a Church,*
*ascribed to Adam of St. Victor (d. 1192)*

IERVSALEM et Sion fíliæ,
coetus omnis fidélis cúriæ,
melos pangant iugis lætítiæ. Alléluia.

2. Christus enim, norma iustítiæ,
matrem nostram despónsat hódie,
quam de lacu traxit misériæ ecclésiam.

3. Hanc sánguinis et aquæ múnere,
dum pendéret in crucis árbore
de próprio prodúxit látere Deus homo.

4. Eua fuit nouérca pósteris,
hæc est mater elécti géneris,
uitæ parens, asylum míseris et tutéla.

5. Hæc est cymba qua tuti uéhimur,
hoc ouíle quo tecti cóndimur,
hæc colúmna qua firmi nítimur uéritatis.

6. Christus iungens nos suis núptiis
recreátos ueris delíciis
interésse fáciat gáudiis electórum.

58

*Sequence for the Dedication of a Church,
ascribed to Adam of St. Victor (d. 1192)*

DAUGHTERS of Jerusalem
and Sion, all the company of
faithful people, sing a hymn
of lasting joy. Alleluia.

2. For Christ, King of justice, this
day has espoused our mother the
Church, whom he saved from the
depth of woe.

3. He, God and man, hanging on the
tree of the cross founded her with
blood and water from his side.

4. Eve was a cruel mother to her
children; the Church is the true mother of the chosen people, giver of life,
refuge & guardian of unhappy man.

5. She is the ship in which we are
borne safely, the fold in which we
are at peace, the column of truth by
which we stand firm.

6. So may Christ, joining us to his
wedding-feast, give us true happi-
ness, inviting us to the joy of his
elect.

59
*Psalm* cxxix *and Responsory for the faithful
departed in the Mozarabic rite*

DE profúndis clamáui ad te, Dómine: *
Dómine, exáudi uocem meam.
2. Fiant aures tuæ intendéntes * in uocem deprecatiónis meæ.
3. Si iniquitátes obseruáueris Dómine, * Dómine, quis sustinébit?
4. Quia apud te propitiátio est: * et propter
legem tuam sustínui te, Dómine.
5. Sustínuit ánima mea in uerbo eius: * speráu-
uit ánima mea in Dómino.
6. A custódia matutína usque ad noctem: *
speret Israel in Dómino.
7. Quia apud Dóminum misericórdia: * et
copiósa apud eum redémptio.
8. Et ipse rédimet Israel, * ex ómnibus iniquitátibus ejus.
V. Réquiem ætérnam dona eis Dómine.
R. Et lux perpétua lúceat eis.

IN loco uíridi Dómine ibi eos cólloca. Super
aquam refectiónis educ ánimas eórum ad
uitam.
V. Réquiem ætérnam dona eis Dómine, et
lux perpétua lúceat eis.
Super aquam refectiónis educ ánimas eórum
ad uitam.

## 59

*Psalm* cxxix *and Responsory for the faithful
departed in the Mozarabic rite*

OUT of the depths I have cried unto
thee, O Lord: Lord hear my voice.
2. Let thine ears be attentive to the
voice of my supplication.

3. If thou, O Lord, shalt observe iniquities,
Lord, who shall endure it?

4. For with thee there is merciful forgiveness:
and by reason of thy law I have waited for
thee, O Lord.

5. My soul hath relied on his word; my soul
hath hoped in the Lord.

6. From the morning watch even until night,
let Israel hope in the Lord.

7. Because with the Lord there is mercy; and
with him plentiful redemption.

8. And he shall redeem Israel from all his iniquities.

V. Eternal rest give unto them, O Lord.

R. And let perpetual light shine upon them.

IN a fertile place, O Lord, there gather
them. By waters of refreshment lead their
souls to life.

V. Eternal rest give unto them, O Lord, and
let perpetual light shine upon them.

By waters of refreshment lead their souls to life.

s

60

*Hymn of the heavenly Jerusalem,*
*by Peter Abelard (d. 1142)*

O QVANTA quália sunt illa sábbata
quæ semper célebrat supérna cúria;
quæ fessis réquies, quæ merces fórtibus
cum erit ómnia Deus in ómnibus.

2. Vere Ierúsalem est illa cíuitas
cuius pax iugis est summa iucúnditas,
ubi non praeuenit rem desidérium,
nec desidério minus est praémium.

3. Illic moléstiis finítis ómnibus
secúri cántica Sion cantábimus,
et iuges grátias de donis grátiæ
beáta réferet plebs tibi Dómine.

4. Illic ex sábbato succédet sábbatum,
perpes lætítia sabbatizántium;
nec ineffábiles cessábunt iúbili
quos decantábimus et nos et ángeli.

5. Nostrum est ínterim mentes erígere
et totis pátriam uotis appétere,
et ad Ierúsalem de Babylónia
post longa régredi tandem exsília.

6. Perénni Dómino perpes sit glória,
ex quo sunt, per quem sunt, in quo sunt ómnia.
Ex quo sunt Pater est, per quem sunt Fílius,
in quo sunt, Patris et Fílii Spíritus.

60

*Hymn of the heavenly Jerusalem,*
*by Peter Abelard (d. 1142)*

WHAT, how great is that day of rest
which the heavenly court ever keeps;
what rest to the weary, what a reward
to the strong, when God shall be all in all.

2. True Jerusalem is that city whose eternal
peace is highest joy, where every wish is satis-
fied, where no wish can exceed what we shall
possess.

3. There all troubles shall be over and we shall
sing the songs of Sion in safety; there the blessed people will give eternal thanks for thy gifts
to thee, O Lord.

4. There day of rest succeeds day of rest in
the unchanging joy of them who keep un-
broken rest; nor will the hymns ever cease
which we with the angels shall sing.

5. Meanwhile we must lift up our hearts, looking eagerly towards our fatherland, hoping at
last to come to Jerusalem after long exile in
Babylon.

6. To the eternal Lord be glory for ever, from
whom and through whom and in whom are
all things. All things from the Father, through
the Son, in the Spirit of the Father and Son.

# COMPLINE FOR SUNDAY

A READER BEGINS: V. Iube, domne, benedícere.

THE BLESSING.

Noctem quiétam, et finem perféctum concédat nobis Dóminus omnípotens. R. Amen.

THE SHORT LESSON. 1 Peter v, 8, 9.

FRATRES: Sóbrii estóte, et uigiláte: quia aduersárius uester diábolus tamquam leo rúgiens círcuit, quærens quem déuoret: cui resístite fortes in fide. Tu autem, Dómine, miserére nobis.

R. Deo grátias.

V. Adiutórium nostrum in nómine Dómini.

R. Qui fecit cælum et terram.

THEN IS SAID SILENTLY:

PATER noster, qui es in cælis, sanctificétur nomen tuum. Aduéniat regnum tuum. Fiat uolúntas tua, sicut in cælo et in terra. Panem nostrum quotidiánum da nobis hódie. Et dimítte nobis débita nostra, sicut et nos dimíttimus debitóribus nostris. Et ne nos indúcas in tentatiónem: sed líbera nos a malo. Amen.

THE HEBDOMADARIUS MAKES THE CONFESSION:

CONFITEOR Deo omnipoténti, beátæ Maríæ semper uírgini, beáto Michaéli archángelo, beáto Ioánni Baptístæ, sanctis apóstolis Petro et Paulo, ómnibus sanctis,

# COMPLINE FOR SUNDAY

A READER BEGINS: V. Pray, sir, a blessing.

THE BLESSING.

The Lord almighty grant us a peaceful night and a perfect end. R. Amen.

THE SHORT LESSON.                    1 Peter v, 8, 9.

BRETHREN, be sober and watch: because your adversary the devil as a roaring lion goeth about seeking whom he may devour: whom resist ye strong in faith. But do thou, O Lord, have mercy on us. R. Thanks be to God.

V. Our help is in the name of the Lord.

R. Who made heaven and earth.

THEN IS SAID SILENTLY:

OUR FATHER, who art in heaven, hallowed be thy name; thy kingdom come; thy will be done on earth as it is in heaven. Give us this day our daily bread. And forgive us our trespasses, as we forgive them that trespass against us. And lead us not into temptation; but deliver us from evil. Amen.

THE HEBDOMADARIUS MAKES THE CONFESSION:

I CONFESS to almighty God, to blessed Mary ever Virgin, to blessed Michael the archangel, to blessed John the Baptist, to the holy apostles Peter and Paul, to all the

et uobis, fratres, quia peccáui nimis cogitatióne, uerbo et ópere: mea culpa, mea culpa,
mea máxima culpa. Ideo precor beátam Maríam semper uírginem, beátum Michaélem
archángelum, beátum Ioánnem Baptístam,
sanctos apóstolos Petrum et Paulum, omnes
sanctos, et uos, fratres, oráre pro me ad
Dóminum Deum nostrum.

THE CHOIR ANSWERS:

Misereátur tui omnípotens Deus, et dimíssis
peccátis tuis, perdúcat te ad uitam ætérnam.
R. Amen.

THEN THE CHOIR REPEATS THE CONFESSION:

CONFITEOR Deo omnipoténti, beátæ
Maríæ semper uírgini, beáto Michaéli
archángelo, beáto Ioánni Baptístæ, sanctis apóstolis Petro et Paulo, ómnibus sanctis,
et tibi, pater, quia peccáui nimis cogitatióne,
uerbo et ópere: mea culpa, mea culpa, mea
máxima culpa. Ideo precor beátam Maríam
semper uírginem, beátum Michaélem archángelum, beátum Ioánnem Baptístam, sanctos apóstolos Petrum et Paulum, omnes
sanctos, et te, pater, oráre pro me ad Dóminum Deum nostrum.

THE HEBDOMADARIUS SAYS:

Misereátur uestri omnípotens Deus, et, dimís-

saints, and to you, brethren, that I have sinned exceedingly in thought, word and deed, through my fault, through my fault, through my most grievous fault. Therefore I beseech the blessed Mary ever Virgin, blessed Michael the archangel, blessed John the Baptist, the holy apostles Peter & Paul, all the saints, and you, brethren, to pray to the Lord our God for me.

THE CHOIR ANSWERS:

May almighty God have mercy on thee, and forgive thee thy sins, and bring thee to life everlasting. R. Amen.

THEN THE CHOIR REPEATS THE CONFESSION:

I CONFESS to almighty God, to blessed Mary ever Virgin, to blessed Michael the archangel, to blessed John the Baptist, to the holy apostles Peter and Paul, to all the saints, and to you, father, that I have sinned exceedingly in thought, word and deed, through my fault, through my fault, through my most grievous fault. Therefore I beseech the blessed Mary ever Virgin, blessed Michael the archangel, blessed John the Baptist, the holy apostles Peter and Paul, all the saints, and you, father, to pray to the Lord our God for me.

THE HEBDOMADARIUS SAYS:

May almighty God have mercy on you, and

sis peccátis uestris, perdúcat uos ad uitam ætérnam. R. Amen.

Indulgéntiam, absolutiónem, et remissiónem peccatórum nostrórum tríbuat nobis omnípotens et miséricors Dóminus. R. Amen.

V. Conuérte nos, Deus salutáris noster.

R. Et auérte iram tuam a nobis.

V. Deus in adiutórium meum inténde.

R. Dómine, ad adiuuándum me festína.

Glória Patri et Fílio et Spirítui sancto.

Sicut erat in princípio, et nunc, et semper, et in sæcula sæculórum. Amen. Allelúia. FROM SEPTUAGESIMA TILL MAUNDY THURSDAY: Laus tibi Dómine, rex ætérnæ glóriæ.

ANT. Miserére. AT EASTERTIDE: ANT. Allelúia.

## Psalm IV

CVM inuocárem exaudíuit me Deus iustítiæ meæ: * in tribulatióne dilatásti mihi.

2. Miserére mei, * et exaudi oratiónem meam.

3. Fílii hóminum úsquequo graui corde? * ut quid dilígitis uanitátem, et quæritis mendácium?

4. Et scitóte quóniam mirificáuit Dóminus sanctum suum: * Dóminus exáudiet me, cum clamáuero ad eum.

5. Irascímini, et nolíte peccáre: * quæ dícitis in

forgive you your sins, and bring you to life everlasting. R. Amen.

May the almighty and merciful Lord grant us pardon, absolution and remission of our sins. R. Amen.

V. Convert us, O God our Saviour.

R. And turn away thine anger from us.

V. O God, come to mine assistance.

R. O Lord, make haste to help me.

Glory be to the Father, and to the Son, and to the Holy Ghost. As it was in the beginning, is now, & ever shall be, world without end. Amen. Alleluia. AFTER SEPTUAGESIMA: Praise be to thee, O Lord, King of everlasting glory.

ANT. Have mercy. AT EASTERTIDE: ANT. Alleluia

### Psalm IV

WHEN I called upon him, the God of my justice heard me: when I was in straits, thou didst set me at liberty.

2. Have mercy on me: and hear my prayer.

3. O ye sons of men, how long will ye be dull of heart? why do ye love vanity, and seek after lying?

4. Know ye also that the Lord hath exalted his holy one: the Lord will hear me when I cry unto him.

5. Be ye angry, and sin not: the things you

T

córdibus uestris, in cubílibus uestris compun-
gímini.
6. Sacrificáte sacrifícium iustítiæ, et speráte in
Dómino. * Multi dicunt: Quis osténdit nobis
bona?
7. Signátum est super nos lumen uultus tui
Dómine: * dedísti lætítiam in corde meo.

8. A fruðtu fruménti, uini, et ólei sui * multi-
plicáti sunt.
9. In pace in idípsum * dórmiam, et requie-
scam:
10. Quóniam tu Dómine singuláriter in spe *
constituísti me.                    Glória Patri.

*Psalm* xc

QVI hábitat in adiutório altíssimi, * in
protéðióne Dei cæli commorábitur.
2. Dicet Dómino: Suscéptor meus es
tu, et refúgium meum: * Deus meus,
sperábo in eum.

3. Quóniam ipse liberáuit me de láqueo uen-
ántium, * et a uerbo áspero.
4. Scápulis suis obumbrábit tibi: * et sub pennis
eius sperábis.
5. Scuto circúmdabit te uéritas eius: * non ti-
mébis a timóre noðúrno.

say in your hearts, be sorry for them upon
your beds.

6. Offer up the sacrifice of justice, and trust in
the Lord. Many say, Who showeth us good
things?

7. The light of thy countenance, O Lord, is
signed upon us: thou hast given gladness in
my heart.

8. By the fruit of their corn, and wine, and oil,
are they multiplied.

9. In peace in the selfsame I will sleep, and I
will rest:

10. For thou, O Lord, alone hast established
me in hope.          Glory be to the Father.

### *Psalm* xc

HE that dwelleth in the help of the most
High, shall abide under the protection
of the God of heaven.

2. He shall say unto the Lord: Thou art mine
upholder, and my refuge: my God, in him will
I trust.

3. For he hath delivered me from the snare of
the hunters, and from the sharp word.

4. He shall overshadow thee with his shoulders:
and under his wings thou shalt trust.

5. His truth shall compass thee with a shield;
thou shalt not be afraid for the terror of the
night.

6. A sagítta uolánte in die, a negótio peram-
bulánte in ténebris : * ab incúrsu, et dæmónio
meridiáno.

7. Cadent a látere tuo mille, et decem míllia a
dextris tuis : * ad te autem non appropinquábit.

8. Verúmtamen óculis tuis considerábis : * et
retributiónem peccatórum uidébis.

9. Quóniam tu es Dómine, spes mea : * altíssi-
mum posuísti refúgium tuum.

10. Non accédet ad te malum : * et flagéllum
non appropinquábit tabernáculo tuo.

11. Quóniam ángelis suis mandáuit de te : * ut
custódiant te in ómnibus uiis tuis.

12. In mánibus portábunt te : * ne forte offéndas
ad lápidem pedem tuum.

13. Super áspidem, et basilíscum ambulábis : *
et conculcábis leónem et dracónem.


14. Quóniam in me speráuit, liberábo eum : *
prótegam eum, quóniam cognóuit nomen
meum.

15. Clamábit ad me, et ego exáudiam eum : *
cum ipso sum in tribulatióne : erípiam eum et
glorificábo eum.

16. Longitúdine diérum replébo eum : * et
osténdam illi salutáre meum.

Glória Patri.

6. For the arrow that flieth in the day, for the plague that walketh in the darkness: for the assault of the evil one in the noonday.

7. A thousand shall fall at thy side, and ten thousand at thy right hand: but it shall not come nigh thee.

8. But with thine eyes shalt thou behold, and shalt see the reward of the wicked.

9. For thou, O Lord, art my hope: thou hast made the most High thy refuge.

10. There shall no evil come to thee: neither shall the scourge come near thy dwelling.

11. For he hath given his angels charge over thee: to keep thee in all thy ways.

12. In their hands they shall bear thee up: lest haply thou dash thy foot against a stone.

13. Thou shalt walk upon the asp and the basilisk: the lion and the dragon shalt thou trample under foot.

14. Because he hath hoped in me, I will deliver him: I will protect him, because he hath known my name.

15. He shall cry unto me, and I will hear him. I am with him in trouble: I will deliver him, and I will glorify him.

16. I will fill him with length of days, and will show him my salvation.

Glory be to the Father.

*Psalm* CXXXIII

ECCE nunc benedícite Dóminum, *omnes serui Dómini.

2. Qui statis in domo Dómini, * in átriis domus Dei nostri.

3. In nóctibus extóllite manus uestras in sancta, * et benedícite Dóminum.

4. Benedícat te Dóminus ex Sion, * qui fecit cælum et terram.

Glória Patri.

ANT. Miserére mihi, Dómine, et exáudi oratiónem meam.

AT EASTERTIDE: ANT. Allelúia, allelúia, allelúia.

HYMN

TE lucis ante términum,
rerum creátor, póscimus,
ut pro tua cleméntia
sis præsul et custódia.

2. Procul recédant sómnia,
et nóctium phantásmata;
hostémque nostrum cómprime,
ne polluántur córpora.

3. Præsta, Pater piíssime,
Patríque compar Vnice,
cum Spíritu Paráclito
regnans per omne sæculum. Amen.

### *Psalm* cxxxiii

BEHOLD, now bless ye the Lord, all ye servants of the Lord.
2. Ye that stand in the house of the Lord, in the courts of the house of our God.
3. Lift up your hands by night to the holy places, and bless ye the Lord.
4. May the Lord bless thee out of Sion, who hath made heaven and earth.
Glory be to the Father.
ANT. Have mercy on me, O Lord, and graciously hear my prayer.
AT EASTERTIDE: ANT. Alleluia, alleluia, alleluia.

### HYMN

NOW with the fast departing light,
Maker of all, we ask of thee,
Of thy great mercy, through the night
Our guardian and defence to be.

2. Far off let idle visions fly;
No phantom of the night molest;
Curb thou our raging enemy,
That we in chaste repose may rest.

3. Father of mercies, hear our cry;
Hear us, O sole-begotten Son,
Who with the Holy Ghost most high,
Reignest while endless ages run. Amen.

FOR CHRISTMAS, CORPUS CHRISTI AND FEASTS
OF THE BLESSED VIRGIN MARY:

3. Iesu, tibi sit glória,
   qui natus es de uírgine,
   cum Pátre et almo Spíritu,
   in sempitérna sæcula.

FOR THE EPIPHANY:

3. Iesu, tibi sit glória,
   qui apparuísti géntibus,
   cum Patre et almo Spíritu,
   in sempitérna sæcula.

AT EASTERTIDE:

3. Deo Patri sit glória,
   et Fílio, qui a mórtuis
   surréxit, ac Paráclito,
   in sempitérna sæcula.

FOR THE ASCENSION:

3. Iesu, tibi sit glória,
   qui uiƈtor in cælum redis,
   cum Patre et almo Spíritu,
   in sempitérna sæcula.

FOR WHITSUNDAY:

3. Deo Patri sit glória,
   et Fílio, qui a mórtuis
   surréxit, ac Paráclito,
   in sæculórum sæcula.

FOR CHRISTMAS, CORPUS CHRISTI AND
FEASTS OF THE BLESSED VIRGIN MARY:
3. Jesus, born of a virgin, glory be to
thee, with the Father and the Holy
Ghost for all ages.

### FOR THE EPIPHANY:

3. Jesus, to thee be glory, who hast
shown thyself to gentiles, with the
Father and Holy Ghost, for all ages.

### AT EASTERTIDE:

3. To God the Father be glory, to
the Son who rose from the dead, to
the Holy Ghost for eternal ages.

### FOR THE ASCENSION:

3. Glory be to thee, O Jesus, return-
ing in triumph to heaven, with the
Father and the Holy Ghost, for ever
and ever.

### FOR WHITSUNDAY:

3. To God the Father be glory, to
the Son who rose from the dead, to
the Holy Ghost, for eternal ages.

v

FOR THE TRANSFIGURATION:

3. Iesu, tibi sit glória,
   qui te reuélas páruulis,
   cum Patre et almo Spíritu,
   in sempitérna sæcula.

FOR THE SEVEN DOLOURS OF THE B. V. MARY:

3. Iesu, tibi sit glória,
   qui passus es pro séruulis,
   cum Patre et almo Spíritu,
   in sempitérna sæcula.

LITTLE CHAPTER.                          Jerem. xiv.

TV autem in nobis es, Dómine, et nomen
sanctum tuum inuocátum est super nos:
ne derelínquas nos, Dómine Deus noster.
R. Deo grátias.

SHORT RESPONSORY.

IN manus tuas, Dómine, * comméndo spíri-
tum meum.
CHOIR. In manus tuas, Dómine, comméndo
spiritum meum.
V. Redemísti nos, Dómine Deus ueritátis.
CHOIR. Comméndo spíritum meum.
Glória Patri et Fílio et Spíritui sancto. [At
Passiontide Gloria Patri is not said.]

FOR THE TRANSFIGURATION:

3. Glory be to thee, O Jesus, who dost show thyself to little ones, with the Father and the Holy Ghost, for ever and ever.

FOR THE SEVEN DOLOURS OF THE B.V.M.:

3. Glory be to thee, O Jesus, who didst suffer for thy servants' sake, with the Father and the Holy Ghost, for ever and ever.

LITTLE CHAPTER.                      Jerem. XIV.

BUT thou, O Lord, art amongst us, and thy holy name is called upon us; forsake us not, O Lord our God.
R. Thanks be to God.

SHORT RESPONSORY.

INTO thy hands, O Lord, I commend my spirit.
CHOIR. Into thy hands, O Lord, I commend my spirit.
V. Thou hast redeemed us, O Lord the God of truth. CHOIR. I commend my spirit.
Glory be to the Father and to the Son and to the Holy Ghost. [At Passiontide Glory be to the Father, &c., is not said.]

CHOIR. In manus tuas, Dómine, comméndo
spíritum meum.
V. Custódi nos, Dómine, ut pupíllam óculi.
R. Sub umbra alárum tuárum prótege nos.

AT EASTERTIDE:

In manus tuas, Dómine, comméndo spíritum
meum. * Allelúia, allelúia.
CHOIR. In manus tuas, Dómine, comméndo
spíritum meum. Allelúia, allelúia.
V. Redemísti nos, Dómine Deus ueritátis.
CHOIR. Allelúia, allelúia.
Glória Patri, et Fílio, et Spíritui sancto.
CHOIR. In manus tuas, Dómine, comméndo
spíritum meum. Allelúia, allelúia.
V. Custódi nos, Dómine, ut pupíllam óculi.
Allelúia.
R. Sub umbra alárum tuárum prótege nos.
Allelúia.
ANT. Salua nos.

SONG OF SIMEON.                          Luke ii.

NVNC dimíttis seruum tuum, Dómine,*
secúndum uerbum tuum in pace:
2. Quia uidérunt óculi mei * salutáre
tuum.
3. Quod parásti * ante fáciem ómnium popu-
lórum.
4. Lumen ad reuelatiónem géntium, *et glóriam plebis tuæ Israel.          Glória Patri.

CHOIR. Into thy hands, O Lord, I commend my spirit.

V. Keep us, O Lord, as the apple of thine eye.

R. Protect us under the shadow of thy wings.

AT EASTERTIDE:

Into thy hands, O Lord, I commend my spirit. Alleluia, alleluia.

CHOIR. Into thy hands, O Lord, I commend my spirit. Alleluia, alleluia.

V. Thou hast redeemed us, O Lord the God of truth. CHOIR. Alleluia, alleluia.

Glory be to the Father, and to the Son, and to the Holy Ghost. CHOIR. Into thy hands, O Lord, I commend my spirit. Alleluia, alleluia.

V. Keep us, O Lord, as the apple of thine eye. Alleluia.

R. Protect us under the shadow of thy wings. Alleluia.

ANT. Save us.

SONG OF SIMEON.                               Luke ii.

NOW thou dost dismiss thy servant, O Lord, according to thy word in peace: 2. Because mine eyes have seen thy salvation.

3. Which thou hast prepared before the face of all people:

4 A light to enlighten the gentiles, and the glory of thy people Israel. Glory be to the Father.

ANT. Salua nos, Dómine, uigilántes, custódi nos dormiéntes; ut uigilémus cum Christo, et requiescámus in pace. AT EASTERTIDE: Allelúia.

*The following prayers are omitted on
Doubles and within Octaves*

KYRIE eléison. Christe eléison. Kyrie eléison.

Pater noster. SILENTLY.

V. Et ne nos indúcas in tentatiónem.

R. Sed líbera nos a malo.

Credo in Deum, etc. SILENTLY.

V. Carnis resurrectiónem.

R. Vitam ætérnam. Amen.

V. Benedíctus es, Dómine Deus patrum nostrórum.

R. Et laudábilis et gloriósus in sæcula.

V. Benedicámus Patrem et Fílium cum sancto Spíritu.

R. Laudémus et superexaltémus eum in sæcula.

V. Benedíctus es, Dómine, in firmaménto cæli.

R. Et laudábilis, et gloriósus, et superexaltátus in sæcula.

V. Benedícat et custódiat nos omnípotens et miséricors Dóminus.

R. Amen.

V. Dignáre, Dómine, nocte ista

R. Sine peccáto nos custodíre.

ANT. Save us, O Lord, when we are awake, and keep us while we sleep, that we may watch with Christ & rest in peace. AT EASTERTIDE: Alleluia.

*The following prayers are omitted on Doubles and within Octaves*

LORD have mercy. Christ have mercy. Lord have mercy.
Our Father, &c. SILENTLY.
V. And lead us not into temptation.
R. But deliver us from evil.
I believe in God, &c. SILENTLY.
V. The resurrection of the body.
R. And life everlasting. Amen.
V. Blessed art thou, O Lord, the God of our fathers.
R. And worthy to be praised & glorious for ever.
V. Let us bless the Father and the Son with the Holy Ghost.
R. Let us praise & exalt him above all for ever.
V. Blessed art thou, O Lord, in the firmament of heaven. R. And worthy to be praised and glorious and exalted above all for ever.
V. May the almighty and merciful Lord bless and keep us.
R. Amen.
V. Vouchsafe, O Lord, this night
R. To keep us without sin.

V. Miserére nostri, Dómine.

R. Miserére nostri.

V. Fiat misericórdia tua, Dómine, super nos.

R. Quemádmodum speráuimus in te.

V. Dómine, exáudi oratiónem meam.

R. Et clamor meus ad te uéniat.

V. Dóminus uobíscum.

R. Et cum spíritu tuo.

Orémus.

VISITA, quæsumus Dómine, habitatiónem istam, et omnes insídias inimíci ab ea longe repélle: angéli tui sancti hábitent in ea, qui nos in pace custódiant; et benedíctio tua sit super nos semper. Per Dóminum nostrum Iesum Christum Fílium tuum: qui tecum uiuit et regnat in unitáte Spíritus sancti Deus, per ómnia sæcula sæculórum.

R. Amen.

V. Dóminus uobíscum.

R. Et cum spíritu tuo.

V. Benedicámus Dómino.

R. Deo grátias.

### THE BLESSING

Benedícat et custódiat nos omnípotens et miséricors Dóminus, Pater et Fílius et Spíritus sanctus.

R. Amen.

V. Have mercy on us, O Lord.
R. Have mercy on us.
V. Let thy mercy, O Lord, be upon us.
R. As we have hoped in thee.
V. O Lord, hear my prayer.
R. And let my cry come unto thee.

V. The Lord be with you.
R. And with thy spirit.
Let us pray.

VISIT, we beseech thee, O Lord, this dwelling, and drive far from it all snares of the enemy: let thy holy angels dwell herein, who may keep us in peace: and let thy blessing be always upon us. Through Jesus Christ our Lord, who liveth and reigneth with thee in the unity of the Holy Ghost, God, world without end.
R. Amen.
V. The Lord be with you.
R. And with thy spirit.
V. Let us bless the Lord.
R. Thanks be to God.

#### THE BLESSING

May the almighty and merciful Lord, Father, Son and Holy Ghost, bless and keep us.
R. Amen.

X

THEN IS SAID THE ANTHEM OF THE BLESSED VIR-
GIN MARY FOR THE SEASON.

### I. FROM ADVENT TO CANDLEMAS:
*By Herimann the Lame, monk of Reichenau*
*(d.* 1054)

ALMA Redemptóris mater, quæ pér-
uia caeli porta manes et stella maris,
succúrre cadénti,
súrgere qui curat, pópulo: tu quæ genuísti,
natúra miránte, tuum sanctum Genitórem.
Virgo prius ac postérius, Gabriélis ab ore
sumens illud aue, peccatórum miserére.

#### IN ADVENT:
V. Angelus Dómini nuntiáuit Maríæ.
R. Et concépit de Spíritu sancto.
Orémus.

GRATIAM tuam, quæsumus Dómine
méntibus nostris infúnde: ut qui, ánge-
lo nuntiánte, Christi Fílii tui incarna-
tiónem cognóuimus, per passiónem eius et
crucem ad resurréctiónis glóriam perducámur.
Per eúmdem Christum Dóminum nostrum.
R. Amen.

#### FROM CHRISTMAS TO CANDLEMAS:
V. Post partum Virgo inuioláta permansísti.
R. Dei génitrix, intercéde pro nobis.

THEN IS SAID THE ANTHEM OF THE BLESSED VIRGIN MARY FOR THE SEASON.

I. FROM ADVENT TO CANDLEMAS:
*By Herimann the Lame, monk of Reichenau*
*(d.* 1054)

HOLY mother of our Redeemer, thou gate leading to heaven and star of the sea; help the falling people who seek to rise, thou who, all nature wondering, didst give birth to thy holy Creator. Virgin always, hearing that greeting from Gabriel's lips, take pity on sinners.

IN ADVENT:
V. The angel of the Lord declared unto Mary.
R. And she conceived of the Holy Ghost.
Let us pray.

POUR forth, we beseech thee, O Lord, thy grace into our hearts, that we to whom the incarnation of Christ thy Son was made known by the message of an angel, may by his passion and cross be brought to the glory of his resurrection. Through the same Christ our Lord. R. Amen.

FROM CHRISTMAS TO CANDLEMAS:
V. After childbirth thou didst remain a pure virgin.
R. Mother of God, pray for us.

Orémus.

DEVS, qui salútis ætérnæ beátæ Maríæ uirginitáte fœcúnda humáno géneri præmia præstitísti: tríbue, quæsumus, ut ipsam pro nobis intercédere sentiámus, per quam merúimus auctórem uitæ suscípere, Dóminum nostrum Iesum Christum Fílium tuum. R. Amen.

II. FROM CANDLEMAS TO EASTER:
*First known in the 12th century*

AVE regína cælórum,
aue dómina angelórum:
salue radix, salue porta,
ex qua mundo lux est orta:
Gaude Virgo gloriósa,
super omnes speciósa,
uale o ualde decóra,
et pro nobis Christum exóra.

V. Dignáre me laudáre te, Virgo sacrata.
R. Da mihi uirtútem contra hostes tuos.
Orémus.

CONCEDE, miséricors Deus, fragilitáti nostræ præsídium: ut qui sanctæ Dei genitrícis memóriam ágimus, intercessiónis eius auxílio a nostris iniquitátibus resurgámus. Per eúmdem Christum Dóminum nostrum. R. Amen.

Let us pray.

OGOD, who by the fruitful virginity of blessed Mary hast given to mankind the rewards of eternal salvation; grant, we beseech thee, that we may experience her intercession for us, through whom we received the author of life, our Lord Jesus Christ, thy Son. R. Amen.

### II. FROM CANDLEMAS TO EASTER:
*First known in the 12th century*

HAIL queen of heaven, hail lady of the angels.
Hail root and gate from which the Light of the world was born.
Rejoice glorious Virgin, fairest of all.
Farewell, most beautiful, and pray for us to Christ.

V. Grant that I may praise thee, O holy Virgin.
R. Give me strength against thine enemies.
Let us pray.

GRANT, O merciful God, help to our weakness, that we who commemorate the holy mother of God, may by the help of her intercession rise from our sins. Through the same Christ our Lord.
R. Amen.

### III. AT EASTERTIDE:
*First known about the year* 1200

REGINA cæli lætáre, allelúia;
quia quem meruísti portáre, allelúia,
resurréxit sicut dixit, allelúia:
Ora pro nobis Deum, allelúia.
V. Gaude et lætáre, uirgo María, allelúia.
R. Quia surréxit Dóminus uere, allelúia.
Orémus.

DEVS, qui per resurrectiónem Fílii tui,
Dómini nostri Iesu Christi, mundum
lætificáre dignátus es: præsta, quæsumus, ut per eius genitrícem uírginem Maríam
perpétuæ capiámus gáudia uitæ. Per eúmdem
Christum Dóminum nostrum.
R. Amen.

### IV. IN THE SEASON AFTER PENTECOST:
*By Herimann the Lame of Reichenau* (*d.* 1054)

SALVE Regina, mater misericórdiæ,
uita, dulcédo et spes nostra, salue.
Ad te clamámus éxsules filii Heuæ.
Ad te suspirámus geméntes et flentes in hac
lacrimárum ualle.
Eia ergo, aduocáta nostra, illos tuos misericór-
des óculos ad nos conuérte.

### III. AT EASTERTIDE:
*First known about the year* 1200

QUEEN of heaven, rejoice, alleluia;
for he whom thou wast chosen to bear,
alleluia; has risen as he said, alleluia;
pray for us to God, alleluia.

V. Rejoice and be glad, O Virgin Mary, alleluia.
R. For the Lord hath risen indeed, alleluia.
Let us pray.

O GOD, who didst vouchsafe to give joy
to the world through the resurrection
of thy Son our Lord Jesus Christ;
grant, we beseech thee, that, through his
mother the Virgin Mary, we may obtain the
joys of everlasting life. Through the same
Christ our Lord. R. Amen.

### IV. IN THE SEASON AFTER PENTECOST:
*By Herimann the Lame of Reichenau* (*d.* 1054)

HAIL, holy queen, mother of mercy,
hail our life, our sweetness & our hope.
To thee do we cry, poor banished children of Eve.
To thee do we send up our sighs, mourning
and weeping in this vale of tears.
Turn then, most gracious advocate, thine eyes
of mercy towards us.

Et Iesum, benedíctum fructum uentris tui,
nobis post hoc exsílium osténde.
O clemens, o pia, o dulcis uirgo María.
V. Ora pro nobis, sancta Dei genitrix.
R. Vt digni efficiámur promissiónibus Christi.
Orémus.

OMNIPOTENS sempitérne Deus, qui
gloriósæ uírginis matris Maríæ corpus
et ánimam, ut dignum Fílii tui habitá-
culum éffici mererétur, Spíritu sancto coope-
ránte præparásti : da ut cuius commemoratióne
lætámur, eius pia intercessióne ab instántibus
malis, et a morte perpétua liberémur. Per eúmdem Christum Dóminum nostrum. R. Amen.

COMPLINE ENDS AS FOLLOWS:
V. Diuínum auxílium máneat semper nobís-
cum. R. Amen.

## BENEDICTION
## OF THE BLESSED SACRAMENT

O Salutaris Hostia (p. 80).
Then is sung an anthem, hymn or litany.
Tantum ergo & the collect of Corpus Christi
(p. 84).
After the Benediction the Divine Praises are
said, and lastly the antiphon Adoremus and
Psalm cxvi are sung as on p. 86.

And after this our exile show unto us the blessed fruit of thy womb, Jesus.

O clement, O loving, O sweet Virgin Mary.

V. Pray for us, O holy mother of God.

R. That we may be made worthy of the promises of Christ.                    Let us pray.

ALMIGHTY and everlasting God, who by the co-operation of the Holy Ghost didst make ready the body and soul of the glorious virgin and mother Mary to be a fit dwelling for thy Son, grant that we, who rejoice in her memory, may be freed from present ills and from eternal death by her prayers. Through the same Christ our Lord. R. Amen.

COMPLINE ENDS AS FOLLOWS:

V. May the divine assistance remain always with us.  R. Amen.

## THE DIVINE PRAISES

BLESSED be God. Blessed be his holy name. Blessed be Jesus Christ, true God and true man. Blessed be the name of Jesus. Blessed be his most Sacred Heart. Blessed be Jesus in the most holy Sacrament of the altar. Blessed be the great mother of God, Mary most holy. Blessed be her holy and immaculate conception. Blessed be the name of Mary, virgin and mother. Blessed be God in his angels and in his saints.

Y

# TE DEVM LAVDAMVS

TE DEVM laudámus, te Dóminum confitémur.

2. Te ætérnum Patrem omnis terra uenerátur.

3. Tibi omnes ángeli, tibi cæli et uniuérsæ potestátes:

4. Tibi chérubim et séraphim incessábili uoce proclamant:

5. Sanctus, sanctus, sanctus, Dóminus Deus Sábaoth.

6. Pleni sunt cæli et terra maiestátis glóriæ tuæ.

7. Te gloriósus apostolórum chorus:

8. Te prophetárum laudábilis númerus:

9. Te mártyrum candidátus laudat exércitus.

10. Te per orbem terrárum sancta confitétur ecclésia.

11. Patrem imménsæ maiestátis.

12. Venerándum tuum uerum et únicum Fílium.

13. Sanctum quoque Paráclitum Spíritum.

14. Tu rex glóriæ, Christe.

15. Tu Patris sempitérnus es Fílius.

16. Tu ad liberándum suscépturus hóminem, non horruísti Vírginis úterum.

17. Tu deuícto mortis acúleo, aperuísti credéntibus regna cælórum.

# TE DEVM LAVDAMVS

WE praise thee, O God, we acknowledge thee to be the Lord.

2. All the earth doth worship thee, the Father everlasting.

3. To thee all angels cry aloud, the heavens and all the powers therein.

4. To thee cherubim and seraphim continually do cry:

5. Holy, holy, holy, Lord God of hosts.

6. Heaven and earth are full of the majesty of thy glory.

7. The glorious choir of the apostles praise thee.

8. The admirable company of the prophets praise thee.

9. The white-robed army of martyrs praise thee.

10. The holy Church throughout all the world doth acknowledge thee,

11. The Father of infinite majesty,

12. Thy adorable, true, and only Son.

13. And the Holy Ghost, the Comforter.

14. Thou art the King of glory, O Christ.

15. Thou art the everlasting Son of the Father.

16. Thou, having taken upon thee to deliver man, didst not disdain the Virgin's womb.

17. When thou hadst overcome the sting of death thou didst open the kingdom of heaven to all believers.

18. Tu ad déxteram Dei sedes in glória Patris.

19. Iudex créderis esse uénturus.

20. [HERE IT IS USUAL TO KNEEL.] Te ergo quæsumus, tuis fámulis súbueni quos pretióso sánguine redemísti.

21. Ætérna fac cum sanctis tuis in glória numerári.

22. Saluum fac pópulum tuum Dómine, et benedic hæreditáti tuæ.

23. Et rege eos et extólle illos usque in ætérnum.

24. Per síngulos dies benedícimus te.

25. Et laudámus nomen tuum in sæculum, et in sæculum sæculi.

26. Dignáre Dómine die isto sine peccáto nos custodíre.

27. Miserére nostri Dómine, miserére nostri.

28. Fiat misericórdia tua Dómine super nos: quemádmodum speráuimus in te.

29. In te Dómine speráui; non confúndar in ætérnum.

ON OCCASIONS OF THANKSGIVING IS ADDED:
V. Benedíctus es, Dómine Deus patrum nostrórum.
R. Et laudábilis et gloriósus in sæcula.

18. Thou sittest at the right hand of God, in the glory of the Father.

19. We believe that thou shalt come to be our Judge.

20. We pray thee, therefore, help thy servants, whom thou hast redeemed with thy precious blood.

21. Make them to be numbered with thy saints in glory everlasting.

22. O Lord, save thy people, and bless thine inheritance.

23. Govern them and lift them up for ever.

24. Day by day we bless thee.

25. And we praise thy name for ever, yea for ever and ever.

26. Vouchsafe, O Lord, this day to keep us without sin.

27. O Lord, have mercy upon us, have mercy upon us.

28. O Lord, let thy mercy be upon us, as we have hoped in thee.

29. O Lord, in thee have I hoped, let me not be confounded for ever.

ON OCCASIONS OF THANKSGIVING IS ADDED:
V. Blessed art thou, O Lord the God of our fathers.
R. And worthy to be praised and glorious for ever.

V. Benedicámus Patrem et Fílium cum sancto Spíritu.

R. Laudémus et superexaltémus eum in sæcula.

V. Benedíctus es, Dómine Deus, in firmaménto cæli.

R. Et laudábilis, et gloriósus, et superexaltátus in sæcula.

V. Dómine, exáudi oratiónem meam.

R. Et clamor meus ad te uéniat.

V. Dóminus uobíscum.

R. Et cum spíritu tuo.

Orémus.

DEVS, cuius misericórdiæ non est númerus, et bonitátis infinítus est thesaúrus, piíssimæ maiestáti tuæ pro collátis donis grátias ágimus, tuam semper cleméntiam exorántes: ut qui peténtibus postuláta concédis, eósdem non déserens, ad præmia futúra dispónas. Per Christum Dóminum nostrum.

R. Amen.


MANE NOBISCVM DOMINE
QVONIAM ADVESPERASCIT

V. Let us bless the Father and the Son with the Holy Ghost.

R. Let us praise and magnify him for ever.

V. Blessed art thou, O Lord, in the firmament of heaven.

R. And worthy to be praised and glorious and exalted for ever.

V. O Lord, hear my prayer.

R. And let my cry come unto thee.

V. The Lord be with you.

R. And with thy spirit.

Let us pray.

O GOD, whose mercies are numberless and the treasure of whose goodness has no end, we give thanks to thy most gracious Majesty for the gifts thou hast bestowed, beseeching thy mercy that, as thou grantest the petitions of them that ask, so, not forsaking them, thou wilt prepare them for rewards to come. Through Christ our Lord. R. Amen.

ABIDE WITH US O LORD
FOR IT IS TOWARD EVENING

DORMIT IN PACE
ADRIANVS A FORTI SCVTO
PRESBYTER
WESTMONASTERIENSIS
QVI NATVS DIE XIV
IANVARII MDCCCLXXIV
ANIMARVM SALVTI
SEDVLO INSERVIENS
AMPLISSIMIS TAMEN
DISCIPLINIS EGREGIE
VACAVIT
OBIIT DIE XI FEBRVARII
MCMXXIII

*Quaerens me sedisti lassus*
*Redemisti crucem passus*
*Tantus labor non sit cassus*

ORA PRO EO

# AFTERWORD

Father Adrian Fortescue, a priest of unique and remarkable talents who truly merited the title of genius, was probably the outstanding scholar among the clergy of the English-speaking world in the first three decades of this century.

He was born on January 14, 1874, to a family of ancient lineage and high position. At the Battle of Hastings in 1066, William the Conqueror was saved from death by Richard le Fort, who interposed his shield between the Norman king and a man about to kill him. The family then took as their motto *Forte scutum salus ducum*—"A strong shield is the safety of leaders"—and it is from this motto the name Fortescue is derived.

Adrian Fortescue entered the Scots' College in Rome in 1891, and in 1894 was enrolled in the theological faculty at Innsbruck University. He was ordained priest by the Prince Bishop of Brixen in 1898, and by 1905 had been awarded three doctorates, a rare achievement.

He was a very talented artist and musician, probably the best calligrapher in Britain, and a brilliant linguist who could preach and write in eleven languages. He was the author of at least thirty books and pamphlets, among which his histories of the Eastern Churches, *The Mass: A Study of the Roman Liturgy,* and *Ceremonies of the Roman Rite Described* are the best known. The latter was the "bible" for masters of ceremonies, and the invariable reaction to a problem in arranging any liturgical ceremony, from the Forty Hours to Pontifical Mass at the Faldstool, was: "Look it up in Fortescue."

Referred to by his friends and parishioners as "the Doctor," Fortescue spent most of his priestly life in Letchworth, Hertfordshire, the world's first "Garden City," based on the philosophy of Ebenezer Howard. Work began in 1903 on what was probably the first completely pre-planned town since Roman times, and the concept was so successful that it has since been taken up throughout the world. The Doctor was appointed "Missionary Rector" of Letchworth in 1907, and offered Mass in a wooden shed near the railway line until the construction of the first church of St. Hugh was completed in 1908 (he would never allow it to be referred to as "St. Hugh's").

The congregation of St. Hugh was probably better instructed in the Catholic religion than any in Europe. Dr. Fortescue took endless pains to ensure that every parishioner understood the Faith thoroughly and was able to play a full and intelligent part in the liturgy. To be present at the Doctor's Mass was an unforgettable experience. He spent hours with his servers before all great feasts, practicing every detail of the ceremony; those of Holy Week in particular

**Adrian Fortescue (1874-1923)**

were carried out with a perfection that brought many visitors to St. Hugh.

In his preaching he eschewed all that smacked of emotionalism. His sermons were short, carefully pre-

pared, and replete with instruction. Only during his
Lenten sermons on the Passion, which attracted non-
Catholics to St. Hugh, did he lay aside his reticence
and speak words that brought tears to the eyes and
won converts to the Faith. He made many converts
at Letchworth and took great pains in their instruction.

The music at St. Hugh was of a uniquely high
standard for a parish church. To be a member of its
choir was to receive a thorough musical education
from the Doctor and his devoted choirmaster, Wilfrid
Willson, whom he appointed as organist in 1908
while still an Anglican. He eventually became a
Catholic, choirmaster and a close friend of the Doctor. Their aim was musical perfection, and they must
have come as near to achieving it as any parish choir
has ever done.

In 1913 Dr. Fortescue compiled for his people
this volume of Latin hymns sung at St. Hugh with
his own English translations. In his preface, he states
that its purpose was to enable those who knew the
tunes to join in the singing, and those who did not
to follow what was being sung. He did not include
the musical notation, as his parishioners would generally have been unable to read plainchant, and would
have picked up the tunes by joining in with the
choir—the way in which every Catholic before the
Second Vatican Council could sing the Latin hymns
at Benediction.

Dr. Fortescue reminded his readers that there has
never been any religious poetry in the world to be

compared with the hymns of the Latin office:

> It would be a disgrace if we Catholics were the
> only people who did not appreciate what is our prop-
> erty. And, from every point of view, we of the old
> Church cannot do better than sing to God as our fa-
> thers sang to Him during all the long ages behind us.
> Nor shall we find a better expression of Catholic piety
> than these words, hallowed by centuries of Catholic
> use, fragrant with the memory of the saints who wrote
> in that golden age when practically the whole of
> Christendom was Catholic.

The norms for music mandated by the Second
Vatican Council conform almost exactly to the pat-
tern established by the Doctor during his fifteen years
at St. Hugh: Gregorian chant as the norm with po-
lyphony by no means excluded. Dr. Fortescue real-
ized, however, that although a good parish choir
could be expected to master the plainchant settings
of the Ordinary of the Mass, the time required each
week to learn the Propers from the *Liber Usualis*
was rather more than an amateur choir was able to
give, and so he adapted, and in some cases composed, simple chants to which parts of the Proper
might be sung.

Despite the explicit command of the the Second
Vatican Council in article 116 of its Liturgy Consti-
tution, the resurgence of Gregorian chant, desired so
earnestly by St. Pius X and implemented so faith-
fully by Dr. Fortescue, has not taken place. The

reverse has happened. The Council referred to the musical tradition of the universal Church as "a treasure of immeasurable value, greater even than that of any other art" (article 112). It commanded that this treasure should be "preserved and fostered with very great care" (article 114). In the English-speaking world, at least, the treasury of Latin music tends to be confined to the concert hall and recordings bought by the million with great enthusiasm by non-Catholics. Dr. Fortescue's book has been republished in the hope of doing at least something to remedy the present situation, in which most Catholics appear quite unaware even of the existence of the musical treasure that is their heritage.

Apart from their unparalleled poetic quality and melodies that appear to have been composed in heaven, the doctrinal content of these hymns will be a revelation to those who pray and study them with devotion and care. In many cases a single hymn will merit hours or more of meditation, either in the Latin original or in the Doctor's prose translation, which has the quality of great poetry and was admired as an example of his finest writing, conforming fully to his own maxim that a good translation should read like an original work.

The book is also an example of superb typography which, inspired by William Morris, was undergoing a renaissance in England at that time, with Bernard Newdigate's Arden Press at Letchworth playing a prominent part. The first edition of this book was set for the Doctor in Caslon type by

Above: The embossed cover for the 1913 edition, by
Stanley Morison. It incorporates a device designed by
Dr. Fortescue and adopted as his *sigillum* (seal) from
1911 onwards, containing the Greek letters IC, XC,
NI, KA—which stand for "Jesus Christ Conquers." This
seal is featured in many of his books and pamphlets.

Newdigate, and printed by his sister on their small press at Astley Cottage in Letchworth. The second edition, of which this is a facsimile, was set in Caslon by Stanley Morison, the finest typographer of his time, and, like Newdigate, a friend and admirer of Dr. Fortescue. It differs from the first edition both in Morison's elegant cover design and in the use of Caslon italic, to which Newdigate did not have access, for the introductions to the hymns. It was printed by the Cambridge University Press to the superlative standard for which it was renowned throughout the world, and the book thus provides the most worthy presentation possible for the sublime hymns that it contains. It has been an eagerly sought and very expensive collector's item for more than half a century, among both Catholic admirers of Dr. Fortescue and non-Catholic students of typography.

In the midst of life this amazing scholar and dedicated pastor was unexpectedly called away. In December 1922, feeling unwell for the first time in his life, he was advised to consult a Harley Street specialist who diagnosed cancer in an advanced stage, and delivered what the Doctor described as his "sentence of death." He returned to his beloved St. Hugh, celebrated all the Christmas offices, made his will, sorted his papers, put the parish records in order for his successor, and preached his final sermon on December 31: "Christ our Friend and Comforter." Before leaving for a hospital in London on January 3, 1923, Dr. Fortescue entered his little church for a long and final farewell. He was seen to kiss fer-

vently the altar on which he had so often offered the
Holy Sacrifice, about which he had written so pro-
foundly. He died on February 11, 1923, less than a
month after his forty-ninth birthday, and despite the
wish of his family that he should be laid to rest
among his ancestors, he chose to be buried among
his parishioners in the cemetery at Letchworth.

It is entirely fitting that in the grave behind his
own is that of his devoted choirmaster, Wilfrid
Willson, and his wife Clare. Upon the Doctor's head-
stone is carved the inscription:

*HIC IACET*
*ADRIANVS A FORTI SCVTO*
*PRESBYTER*
*WESTMONASTERIENSIS*
*BEATEM SPEM EXPECTANS*

Around the tomb itself are the inspired and in-
spiring words of Psalm 25, verse 8, which express
the motivating force of his entire priestly life:

*DOMINE, DILEXI DECOREM DOMVS TVAE,*
*ET LOCVM HABITATIONIS GLORIAE TVAE.*

I wish to acknowledge the help given to me in
preparing this Afterword by Mr. Adrian Willson,
who is the eldest son of Dr. Fortescue's choir direc-
tor, and is named after the Doctor. I am particularly
grateful to him for the photograph of Dr. Fortescue
that appears in this Afterword. I must also thank Mr.

John Scruby, the historian of Letchworth, for his expert advice on the typographical history of the book.

*Michael Davies*
*January 14, 1994,*
*the 120th anniversary of the*
*birth of Dr. Adrian Fortescue,*
*Feast of St. Hilary of Poitiers,*
*Bishop and Doctor*